MY BACKPACK IS HEAVIER THAN YOURS

I0155516

JUST RISE ED
PUBLICATION

www.JustRiseEd.com
DrEdwinGarciaJr@JustRiseEd.com

MY BACKPACK IS HEAVIER THAN YOURS: The Plight of Marginalized Students.

Copyright © 2023 by Dr. Edwin Garcia, Jr.

Cover and images copyright © 2023 by Dr. Edwin Garcia, Jr.

ISBN: 979-8-9881936-0-9 (Paperback)
ISBN: 979-8-9881936-2-3 (Hardcover)
ISBN: 979-8-9881936-1-6 (eBook)

Library of Congress Control Number: 2023907117

Just Rise Ed LLC
www.JustRiseEd.com
DrEdwinGarciaJr@JustRiseEd.com

JUST RISE ED
PUBLICATION

Dedication

This book is dedicated to all the students, parents, and educators I have been blessed and honored to work with and for. Thank you to the educators I had as a student for helping me overcome a failed system. You will all forever hold a piece of my heart.

To all those people who told me I couldn't, I just did!

To all the marginalized students who have overcome and those still fighting – know that Dr. Garcia will always fight for you. You can and will reach your potential if you believe in yourself as much as I do.

Thank you to my friends, family, and colleagues who supported and continue supporting me with all my crazy ideas and dreams.

Mami and Papi, there will never be enough words for me to express how grateful I am.

I certainly could not have completed this book without the support of my wife, Jessica Torres-Garcia. You held down the fort with our beautiful children, Mykah, Liam, our angel Makaylah, Joshua, and Paris, while I went after 4 degrees, including a Doctorate. I could not have done any of this without you.

Finally, I dedicate this book to my children. Every day I strive to ensure you have the opportunities I didn't, and I wake up with one goal: to help this world get a little better every day for you.

MY BACKPACK IS HEAVIER THAN YOURS

The Plight of Marginalized Students.

DR. EDWIN GARCIA JR.

Table of Contents

Introduction

A Personal Journey to Shed Light on the Plight of Marginalized Students.

Born to teenage parents and having lived in poverty for most of my childhood, I have faced many challenges shaping my perspective on life and education. As an educator deeply committed to the success and well-being of my students, I have had the privilege of witnessing countless moments of growth, discovery, and resilience. Yet, despite the many triumphs, it has become increasingly apparent that not all students are afforded the same opportunities to thrive. This book, "MY BACKPACK IS HEAVIER THAN YOURS: The Plight of Marginalized Students," is born out of my firsthand experiences, the stories of the students and friends I've encountered, and the realization that we must do more to support those who face unique and often overwhelming challenges in their pursuit of education.

Throughout this book, the term "marginalized students" will be used to describe a diverse group of individuals who are often disadvantaged or underrepresented in the education system, including students of color, students from low socioeconomic backgrounds, students with disabilities, English Language Learners, LGBTQ+ students, students from religious minorities, and others who may face unique challenges or barriers in their educational journey.

Growing up, I often felt as though I didn't belong, grappling with the weight of the expectations and judgments placed upon me. My experiences have instilled in me a deep understanding of the barriers that marginalized students face and a passion for fostering change in the education system. Yet, despite the new heights I reach every day, I cannot help but acknowledge that I am one of the lucky ones.

This book does not purport to cover all the challenges that marginalized students face, nor does it claim to hold all the answers. Instead, it aims to continue the difficult conversations that many before me have started, bringing those discussions closer together and shedding light on the significant barriers that marginalized students currently face in our education system. Drawing from a wealth of research, personal narratives, and insights from fellow educators, friends, parents, and students, this book endeavors to provide a better understanding of the complexities and nuances of these challenges and offer some potential solutions.

Throughout the chapters, you will find moments of reflection designed to encourage all stakeholders - educators, policymakers, parents, and community members - to consider their roles in fostering a more inclusive and equitable learning environment. We will explore the systemic barriers and biases that undermine the potential of marginalized students and discuss practical next steps for various stakeholders to make a difference. Toward the end of the book, we will dive through some deep reflection questions, finishing with some next steps the different stakeholder groups can take to improve our education system for all. While the primary audience of this book is educators and decision-makers, all stakeholders can benefit from its content.

As we embark on this journey together, I sincerely hope that "MY BACKPACK IS HEAVIER THAN YOURS" will serve as a catalyst for change, inspiring all of us to recognize the weight of the backpacks carried by marginalized students and to work collaboratively toward lightening their burdens. Only through empathy, understanding, and collective action can we ensure every student has the opportunity to succeed, regardless of the unique challenges or barriers they face in their educational journey.

Prologue

I am Still a Kid.

My name is a puzzle, a tongue-twisting affair.

No one cared enough to pronounce it right; no one would dare.

It's just a small thing, but it felt like a blow.

A reminder that I was different, an outsider, a foe.

Trying to keep up with the others, no thanks to politics.

Their backpacks filled with books, while mine was filled with bricks.

I am a student of color, poor, and struggling.

Every day, I face challenges; my dreams I am juggling.

Trying to fit in, trying to belong.

But the walls seemed too high, the climb too long.

So I acted out for attention, for someone to see.

But all they saw was a troublemaker, not a kid just trying to be.

Trying to be a good student, trying to learn and grow.

But no one believed in me; they just wanted me to go.

Go back to where I came from, where my name was more than a token.

But I stayed; I persevered, though my heart was broken.

Broken by the indifference, the ignorance, the hate.

I was still a kid; was I not allowed mistakes?

But no one seemed to see that; no one seemed to care.

Until one day, a teacher came, and my world became more fair.

She pronounced my name right, and it was like music to my ears.

And suddenly, I had a voice, a reason to be here.

She saw beyond my struggles, and she saw the good in me.

And for the first time, I believed that I could be free.

Free from the chains of doubt and fear.

Free to dream, free to persevere.

Thanks to that one teacher who believed in me.

I can see a future, where I can be all I want to be.

So let me make mistakes; let me stumble and fall.

For I am still a kid, trying to find my way through it all.

And with the support of a teacher who believes,

I can conquer anything, and achieve all my dreams.

Have you ever considered how something as simple as pronouncing a person's name could impact your relationship with them?

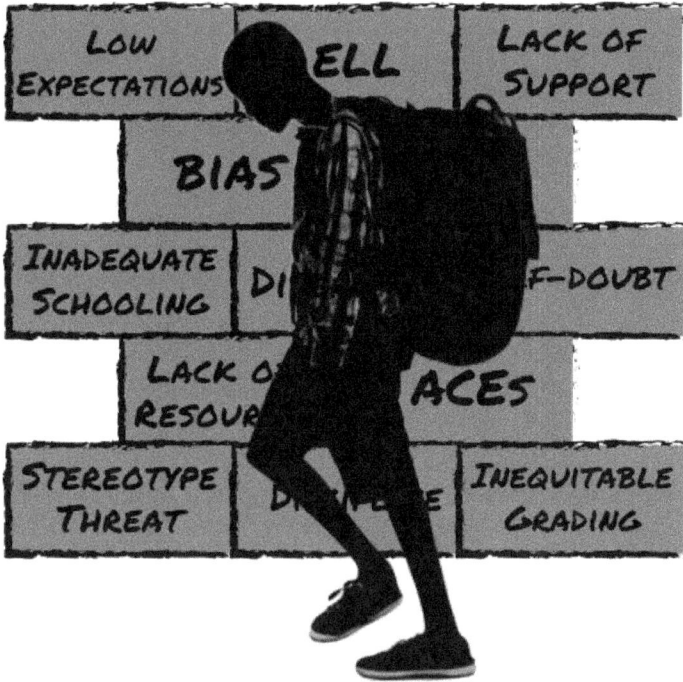

Chapter 1: What's in My Backpack?

My Backpack

I was primarily raised by my fierce and determined Latina teen mother. I grew up witnessing the harsh realities of a life filled with obstacles and hardships. I grew up in a world that often felt unkind and unforgiving—a young boy of color, born to teenage parents struggling to find their way. My parents were high school dropouts and did their best to provide for their children, but we relied on government assistance and food stamps to make ends meet. I often felt the weight of judgmental stares from strangers as my mother used the colorful government-provided food stamps at the grocery store checkout, a silent reminder of the barriers that society placed upon me, my family, and people like us.

Even with government assistance, our struggles often persisted, no matter how hard my mom worked. We had to heat our home a few times using the gas oven because the electricity was out. The government assistance often provided is barely enough for far too many, and sometimes more is needed. I grew up knowing what it was like to get Christmas gifts from the Salvation Army. I remember like it was yesterday, looking at the big-name clothes and sneakers, not choosing what I really wanted because we did not always have. I did not want to add to the burden my parents shouldered.

The schools I attended were underfunded and lacked resources, yet I persevered. In the sixth grade, I faced the inconsistency of having four different teachers throughout the year but still achieved straight A's. Despite my academic success, I was met with disbelief by those who were supposed to praise and support me when I scored high on a state math test, only to be placed in a transitional class rather than an honors class. With no computer at home and limited access to technology at school well into my teen years, I relied on borrowed encyclopedias from a kind neighbor who had acquired them through a payment plan and old, outdated books.

As I grew older, I remained unaware of the possibilities that higher education could offer. No one I could remember at school had ever mentioned the prospect of college or how I could pay for it. Eventually, I enrolled in community college, only to be placed in remedial courses. This further fueled my frustration with the educational system. Growing up poor, I had no genuine concept of making a livable wage. I only knew what I needed to keep surviving. To me, surviving was good enough. The minute I got what I thought was a real job, with the frustration of a failed system pushing me, I dropped out of college only months after I started.

After ten years had passed and the birth of my first son, I decided to rewrite my story. I returned to school and earned a bachelor's degree, then left a comfortable tech job to give back to the school district that had failed to recognize and instill in me my potential. Driven by a desire to show other children like me that they could achieve, the college dropout earned two master's degrees and then a Doctor of Education in Curriculum and Instruction, graduating summa cum laude.

It wasn't easy, but I was determined to succeed despite the challenges. I consider myself one of the lucky ones. Looking back, I'm proud of how far I've come, and I know that my experiences have made me stronger and more resilient. I would not wish my struggles on anyone.

The story of struggle sometimes ends differently for others than my story. I know people whose stories were similar, better, and worst, who did not make it. Many of my friends and neighbors did not escape poverty and still rely on the failed system today. They say it takes a village, and I was lucky to have educators and mentors around me who understood the assignment. The system more than not fails people like me.

Many of our students are walking around with the heavyweight brought on by the bricks of adversity in their backpacks. They carry this extra weight around them all day. My personal and professional experiences are reinforced by the research that shows that students often mask their pain, frustration, and anxiety with walls of aggression, substance abuse, risk-taking behaviors, withdrawal, and disrespectful behaviors (Schwartz et al., 2012; Turner and Butler, 2003; Youniss, McLellan, and Yates, 1997). As educators, we must not add to our students' adversities. Still, we should look to lighten or liberate them of their burdens whenever we can.

What Do Our Students Carry in Their Backpacks?

In the pursuit of academic excellence, marginalized students are confronted by a labyrinth of external and internal challenges, which often intertwine to create an impenetrable barrier to success. Envision these challenges as burdensome bricks carried within our students' backpacks, with some bearing a heavier load than their peers, weighed down in the race for achievement. As educators, we must confront the harsh reality that, while our hearts may yearn to alleviate the weighty burdens our students bear, there are times when such a task transcends our capabilities. This book was not composed to mandate the removal of their burdens, though our moral compass implores us to do so when possible. Instead, it serves as an impassioned plea for educators to acknowledge our students' struggles and diligently ensure that we do not inadvertently add our bricks to their heavy backpacks. That we take the time to understand these challenges and do what we can to help them succeed in light of them.

External challenges:

1. Lack of resources: Marginalized students may not have access to the same resources as their wealthier peers, such as private tutoring, advanced textbooks, or expensive technology. This can put them at a disadvantage in terms of academic achievement.

2. Inadequate schooling: Schools in low-income areas are often underfunded and understaffed, resulting in less access to quality education. This can lead to lower test scores, less college preparedness, and fewer advanced coursework opportunities.

3. Discrimination: Students of color may experience discrimination based on race or ethnicity, impacting their academic performance. They may also face implicit biases from educators and peers, resulting in lower expectations and fewer opportunities. Sometimes discrimination stems from friend and family relations.

Internal challenges:

1. Stereotype threat: Marginalized students may feel pressure to live up to negative stereotypes often associated with their race, ethnicity, or familial. This can lead to anxiety, which can negatively impact academic performance.

2. Self-doubt: Marginalized students may doubt their ability to succeed academically, especially if they don't see others like themselves achieving at high levels. This can lead to a lack of motivation and lower academic performance.

3. Lack of support: Students who are often marginalized may have different levels of support from their families and communities than their peers. This can result in a lack of resources, mentoring, and guidance, making it harder for them to succeed academically.

4. Adverse Childhood Experiences (ACEs): Marginalized students are more likely to experience ACEs, which can have a negative impact on their academic achievement. ACEs include poverty, violence, and neglect, leading to toxic stress, changes in brain development, and behavioral and emotional problems. These experiences can make it more difficult for students to learn and succeed in school.

5. English language learners (ELLs): Marginalized students may also experience challenges when learning English as a second language (ESL). ELLs often face additional barriers to academic success compared to their native-English-speaking peers.

The struggles marginalized students endure in their quest for academic success demand a kaleidoscope of solutions as multifaceted as the challenges themselves. Our response must encompass the enhancement of educational access and the dismantling of discrimination and prejudice. We must foster mentorship and support, cultivate resilience through trauma-informed practices, and champion mental health services. Additionally, we must strive to reshape societal perspectives and forge havens of safety and encouragement for these students. Attempting to resolve a single issue is akin to driving with a solitary wheel in motion – it may propel us forward, but can we truly reach our desired destination with the urgency these students deserve?

Lack of Resources

Marginalized students often need access to resources that can support their academic achievement. According to the National Center for Education Statistics (2021), students from low-income families are less likely to have access to resources such as high-quality preschool programs, advanced coursework, and technology. In addition, they may lack access to essential resources such as adequate nutrition, healthcare, and stable housing, which can also impact their academic success.

Addressing the lack of resources among marginalized students requires a comprehensive approach that addresses the underlying causes of poverty and supports affected students. This can include policy interventions, such as increasing funding for schools in low-income areas and expanding access to early childhood education programs (National Academies of Sciences, Engineering, and Medicine, 2019). It can also involve providing resources and support within schools, such as free or reduced-price meals, tutoring and mentoring programs, and access to technology and other educational resources. Whatever approach is taken should be done with our students in mind and with the intention of meeting them where they are. Some of our neediest students are unable to participate in tutoring services because they have to work so their families can pay essential bills, including the food they eat. Sometimes they have to take care of younger siblings because mom and/or dad have two or three jobs. In this case, tutoring directly before or after school would be an example of a solution that does not meet their needs.

Additionally, schools must create a culture of inclusivity and support that recognizes marginalized students' unique challenges. This can involve adopting culturally responsive instructional practices and providing professional development for educators in addressing issues of equity and social justice in the classroom (Gorski, 2017). The approach chosen should not be a one-and-done event; it needs to be a process that happens over time and is ever-evolving.

Inadequate Schooling

Students who belong to marginalized communities are frequently subjected to substandard schooling, which can have an adverse effect on their academic performance. The report from the National Center for Education Statistics (2021) says that schools in low-income areas have fewer resources and experienced educators, as well as higher rates of teacher turnover. High teacher turnover rates result in large classes, even when our students sit in front of a substitute for weeks or months. The substitutes usually have little to no adequate content knowledge. This can result in ineffective instruction, lower academic standards, and a lack of support for our students.

Addressing inadequate schooling for marginalized students requires a comprehensive approach that addresses the underlying causes of educational inequity and supports affected our students. One part of the approach is providing additional resources to schools in low-income areas, such as funding technology and instructional materials and increasing teacher salaries to attract and retain experienced educators (National Academies of Sciences, Engineering, and Medicine, 2019). In addition, schools can implement evidence-based interventions such as high-quality early childhood education programs and afterschool programs that provide academic and social support for students (Duncan & Magnuson, 2013). Investing in programs to recruit and retain teachers must also be a priority, especially trying to recruit teachers who look like our students.

Another strategy is to provide targeted support for our students who are most at risk of falling behind, such as English Language Learners (ELLs) and our students with disabilities. This can involve providing additional resources such as language support services, special education services, and individualized tutoring and mentoring (National Center for Education Statistics, 2021). Providing support through information and workshops to our families with these students is also essential. Support from a family can sometimes mean that families do not have to be able to help with the content being taught. Sometimes sufficient support comes from just checking in with our students, but this is not widely known.

Schools can work to create a culture of high expectations and support for all students. This can involve adopting evidence-based practices such as differentiated instruction in addition to the culturally responsive instructional practices addressed early. Adopting these practices must include a professional development series for staff to be well-versed in these practices.

Discrimination

Our marginalized students also face discrimination, which can impede their academic performance, leading to adverse outcomes. Discrimination can take many forms, such as racial or ethnic bias, economic discrimination, religious discrimination, or discrimination based on gender or sexual orientation. A little-known form of discrimination is familial discrimination for students who are friends or relatives of previously known students. I have witnessed how a student having the same last name as another can trigger discrimination in school staff. According to a report from the National Center for Education Statistics (2021), students from low-income families are more likely to experience discrimination and bias from their peers and educators.

Addressing discrimination among marginalized students requires an intricate approach that addresses systemic inequality, creates a culture of inclusivity and respect within schools, and provides targeted support for affected students. One direction is to provide training and support for teachers and school administrators on addressing equity and social justice issues in the classroom, such as adopting culturally responsive instructional practices and supporting students experiencing discrimination or bias (Gorski, 2017). This approach requires more than just learning certain practices and implementing them. It requires a look into the mirror to gain a deep understanding of our own biases.

Another approach is to create safe and inclusive learning environments that promote diversity and respect for all students. Additionally, the approach should involve implementing anti-bullying policies and providing opportunities for our students to learn about different cultures and perspectives (National Center for Education Statistics, 2021). Schools can also work to create supportive networks for marginalized students, such as mentorship programs and peer support groups. More times than not, an intentional educational approach is nonexistent when it is all that is needed.

Addressing discrimination among marginalized students requires addressing systemic inequality and promoting policies that support economic and social mobility. Advocacy efforts can focus on addressing the root causes of poverty and inequality, including inadequate housing, limited access to healthcare, and low-quality education. Creating partnerships between the school and other entities can be a great way to strengthen advocacy and get the resources needed for systemic change.

Stereotype Threat

Marginalized students may also experience stereotype threat, the fear of being judged or mistreated based on a negative stereotype. Stereotype threat can lead to reduced academic performance, increased stress and anxiety, and lower academic aspirations (Steele, 1997).

Addressing stereotype threats among marginalized students requires creating a supportive and inclusive learning environment that promotes a growth mindset and values diversity. According to a study by Walton and Cohen (2011), interventions that promote a growth mindset can help reduce stereotype threat and improve academic performance among low-income students. One approach is to provide our students with opportunities to learn about and discuss stereotype threat and strategies for managing it. For example, educators can incorporate lessons on stereotype threat and growth mindset into their curriculum and provide students with tools for managing stress and anxiety (Cohen et al., 2009).

Like the other challenges students face, creating a supportive and inclusive classroom environment that values diversity and promotes positive social identity is needed. By creating a culture that celebrates the diversity of our students, educators can help to mitigate the effects of stereotype threat. A study by Cohen et al. (2006) found that when students perceived their school environment as supportive of diversity, they were less likely to experience stereotype threat. Students can be encouraged to engage in positive self-affirmation exercises, such as writing about their personal

12

values or strengths, to reduce negative stereotypes' impact on their academic performance. The same study by Cohen et al. (2006) found that self-affirmation exercises helped to minimize the adverse effects of stereotype threat on academic performance.

Another way to address stereotype threat by boosting social identity is for schools to provide positive role models for our students from marginalized groups. A study by Good et al. (2012) found that exposure to successful role models from one's ethnic group helped to reduce the effects of stereotype threat on academic performance. By highlighting the achievements of individuals from diverse backgrounds, educators can help to counter negative stereotypes and inspire our students to achieve their goals.

Self-Doubt

Marginalized students may experience self-doubt, negatively affecting their academic performance and overall well-being. Self-doubt can arise from various factors, including a lack of confidence in their abilities, negative experiences or feedback, and comparison with peers who may have more resources or advantages (Cassady & Johnson, 2002). Educators can often exacerbate this through microaggressions that are intentional and unintentional.

Providing our students with opportunities for positive feedback, mentorship, and skill-building is vital to addressing self-doubt among marginalized students. According to a study by Dweck (2006), promoting a growth mindset can help students develop a more positive attitude toward learning and overcome self-doubt.

One approach is providing our students with regular feedback and encouragement, highlighting their strengths and progress. This can involve providing specific and constructive feedback on their assignments and acknowledging their efforts and achievements in class (Cassady & Johnson, 2002). Emphasizing the importance of effort and persistence can significantly reduce self-doubt. This can involve providing students with opportunities to develop their skills and interests and encouraging them to view challenges and setbacks as opportunities for growth and learning (Dweck, 2006).

Another approach is to provide our students with mentorship and role models who can provide guidance and support. For example, schools can partner with community organizations or businesses to provide students with mentorship opportunities or offer programs that connect students with successful alums or professionals in their fields of interest (Bettinger & Baker, 2011). It is not enough for our students to see people who look like them in the curriculum. Developing authentic relationships with mentors who look like them strengthens the positive perception they need to reduce self-doubt.

Lack of Support

Marginalized may lack support from their families and communities, negatively impacting their academic achievement and well-being. Lack of support can arise from various factors, including limited access to academic and emotional resources and a lack of supportive relationships with family and peers (Kim & Hwang, 2018).

It is vital to give marginalized students access to more than just academic resources to address the lack of support among marginalized students. We must also give them emotional resources and opportunities to have supportive relationships. Schools can and often provide academic support through tutoring programs, study groups, and access to high-quality, up-to-date educational resources such as textbooks and technology (Kim & Hwang, 2018). Our students can also be given something a little more. We can provide them to provide emotional support through counseling services, mental health programs, and peer support groups (Kim & Hwang, 2018). Without the assistance of the school or district, our marginalized students do not always have access to these services.

Family and community involvement also play crucial roles in supporting marginalized students' backgrounds. Schools can involve families and community members in the educational process by organizing parent-teacher conferences, community engagement events, and volunteer opportunities (Kim & Hwang, 2018). These efforts can create a more supportive and connected environment for marginalized students. They can also allow our students to express themselves and feel valued. Enabling students to exhibit their learning and acquire knowledge together with their family members demonstrates that they are valued. This approach also allows families to provide support beyond the conventional report card nights. Often, families are unsure how they can support their students.

Addressing the lack of support among marginalized students requires recognizing and addressing the systemic barriers that contribute to educational inequality—advocating for policies that promote equity and access to resources, such as increased funding for low-income schools and programs that support the needs of marginalized students (Reardon, 2011). If we do not invest in our students as children, it will cost us more when they are adults. Think of all the innovation and knowledge lost over the years through our systematic oppression.

Adverse Childhood Experiences (ACEs)

Marginalized are also at higher risk for experiencing Adverse Childhood Experiences (ACEs), which can negatively impact their academic achievement and overall well-being. ACEs can include a range of traumatic experiences, such as abuse, neglect, household dysfunction, and community violence (Anda et al., 2006).

Addressing the impact of ACEs on marginalized students is essential. Schools can implement trauma-informed practices and provide students access to supportive resources. Trauma-informed practices can be complex and should be implemented after extensive research and professional development. Schools can provide professional development to teachers and staff on trauma-informed practices. This includes training on the impact of trauma on our students, identifying trauma symptoms, and responding to trauma in a supportive and empathetic way. A study by Kataoka et al. (2013) found that providing professional development on trauma-informed practices to teachers and staff improved students' mental health outcomes.

Trauma-informed practices involve creating a safe and supportive student environment and responding to their needs sensitively and compassionately (National Child Traumatic Stress Network, n.d.). Schools should create a safe and supportive environment that promotes positive relationships, student engagement, and social-emotional learning. This includes providing opportunities for our students to build positive relationships with educators and peers, creating a calm and predictable learning environment, and using restorative practices to address conflicts. A study by Kostelnik et al. (2016) found that creating a trauma-informed school environment improved students' social-emotional well-being and academic achievement.

Schools can provide our students access to supportive resources through counseling services, mental health programs, and peer support groups (Kim & Hwang, 2018). Schools can use screening and assessment tools to identify students who may have experienced trauma and need additional support. This includes using trauma-specific screening tools, such as the Adverse Childhood Experiences (ACEs) questionnaire, and ongoing assessments to monitor students' mental health and academic progress. Schumacher et al. (2018) found that screening and assessment tools helped identify students who needed additional support and improved their mental health outcomes.

Community and agency partnerships are integral to addressing many of our students' challenges. Schools can engage families and communities in trauma-informed practices to create a more holistic approach to supporting our students. This includes involving families in school decision-making, providing resources and support for families, and building partnerships with community organizations. Cross et al. (2018) found that engaging families and communities in trauma-informed practices improved students' social-emotional well-being and academic achievement. Additionally, schools can work with community organizations to provide wrap-around services that address the various needs of students and their families, such as housing, healthcare, and food assistance (Kim & Hwang, 2018).

English Language Learners (ELLs)

English language learners (ELLs) face unique challenges that can impact their academic achievement. These challenges include limited English proficiency, difficulty understanding academic language, and cultural differences. Studies have shown that providing ELLs with language support through explicit instruction in academic English can help improve their academic achievement (Gersten et al., 2006). Support for English Language

Learners (ELLs) is essential for ensuring our students can access academic content and succeed in school.

Educators should use instructional strategies such as graphic organizers, word walls, and sentence starters to support ELLs' language development (Thompson & Vaughn, 2002). In addition, educators can provide ELLs with opportunities to practice their language skills, such as through small group discussions and writing assignments (Scarcella & Oxford, 1992). Schools can provide academic support beyond regular instruction to ELLs to help them succeed in their coursework. This includes providing extra support in areas where ELLs may struggle, such as reading comprehension and vocabulary development.

Culturally responsive teaching can also help address the unique challenges faced by ELLs. This approach should consider ELLs' cultural backgrounds and experiences and use this knowledge to inform instruction. Some effective strategies for promoting cultural responsiveness in the classroom are utilizing bilingual materials and aides, including diverse perspectives and experiences in lesson plans, and creating space for our students to express their cultural traditions and perspectives. These approaches can help create an inclusive and supportive learning environment for all students. Creating a welcoming and inclusive environment, promoting cross-cultural understanding and respect, and providing opportunities for ELLs to share their culture and experiences are essential. Frequently, ELL students are pushed to conform to the identity of their new home and forgo their own identity. Creating an inclusive environment allows them to assimilate into their new home and be who they are. A study by Siwatu (2016) found that creating a positive school culture improved ELL students' academic achievement.

Schools can also provide additional resources to support ELLs, such as tutoring in their native language, translation services, and after-school programs. These resources can help ELLs and their families navigate the education system and support academic success (Suárez-Orozco & Suárez-Orozco, 2001). Many families I have spoken to throughout the years find navigating their new home's education system challenging. The partnership between home and school is critical to a child's success, and removing this barrier will undoubtedly have positive consequences. By addressing ELLs' unique challenges and providing the necessary support, educators and schools can help ELLs succeed academically and improve their well-being.

Sometimes, the most powerful support we can give is the simple act of listening with an open heart and an empathetic ear.

Chapter 2: Part of the Problem or the Solution

Do You Contribute to the Weight in My Backpack?

When I decided to shift careers from Information Technology to Education, I sought the wisdom of numerous friends and family members. Two pivotal questions guided my transition into this new role and field:

1. What qualities define exceptional educators?
2. What sets apart those educators who leave a lasting impression from those who fade into the background?

My Backpack is Heavier Than Yours

As I conversed with individuals from diverse backgrounds, a common theme emerged. How people make us feel determines whether they remain etched in our minds or become a vague recollection in our memories. We all recall the teachers and educators who made us feel valued and capable, even if they were strict. Conversely, we remember those who caused us pain. My fourth-grade teacher's image remains vivid in my mind, and I still remember her name, whereas my fifth-grade teacher has all but vanished from my memory. The Vice Principal and Assistant Superintendent from my elementary school are still pretty clear in my mind, probably because I remember them being present and welcoming. However, I find it difficult to remember my elementary school Principal.

One particular story that was shared with me revealed the power of a teacher's words in shaping a student's future. A friend initially chose not to attend college after high school, partly because his counselor advised him that college was not the right path for him. However, a transformative moment occurred when his English teacher encouraged him during high school graduation. Despite not earning an A in her class, she praised him as the best writer among her students that year, describing his ability to craft heartfelt stories as unparalleled. She urged him to concentrate on his potential rather than the limitations others imposed on him. This teacher's faith in his abilities motivated him to enroll in college the following spring. Today, more than two decades later, my friend holds two master's degrees and serves as a Regional Vice President of Marketing for a global company.

The power of a single educator's belief in a student's potential cannot be underestimated.

In education, marginalized students are often perceived through lenses that fail to capture their authentic experiences. As adults, our personal biases can lead us to underestimate the struggles faced by our students, ultimately limiting their potential. Our words and actions have a more profound impact than we care to realize or wish to acknowledge. How many students have traversed the halls of our schools or the confines of our classrooms only to be met with negativity rather than encouragement? As educators, it is our duty to ensure that we do not add to the burdens our students carry. Sometimes, the mere act of choosing the right words can make a world of difference. All it takes is one person who genuinely believes in a student to ignite a transformative spark.

Educators serve as crucial pillars in the scaffolding of student success. We must remain vigilant against practices or behaviors obstructing a student's progress. The following strategies can empower educators to champion academic achievement without inadvertently hindering their students:

1. Build positive relationships with students: Educators who build positive relationships with our students are more likely to create a supportive learning environment and foster a sense of belonging among our students. Positive relationships can improve student motivation, engagement, and academic achievement (Roorda et al., 2011).

2. Use culturally responsive instructional strategies: Incorporating culturally responsive instructional strategies into classrooms can lead to a stronger connection between educators and students from various backgrounds. Research has shown that implementing culturally responsive instructional practices can improve academic achievement among students from diverse backgrounds (Ladson-Billings, 2019). These instructional strategies involve using culturally relevant instructional materials, welcoming and inclusive classroom environments, and incorporating students' cultural backgrounds and experiences into the curriculum.

3. Provide frequent and constructive feedback: Providing our students with regular and constructive feedback is an effective way for educators to support their learning and boost academic achievement. The feedback should be actionable and provide specific comments highlighting their strengths, weaknesses, and areas of improvement. Providing opportunities for students to reflect on their learning also contributes to their growth and development (Hattie & Timperley, 2007).

4. Set high expectations for all students: Creating a conducive learning environment that fosters high expectations can significantly contribute to academic achievement and assist our students in fulfilling their potential. This can be achieved by offering students challenging assignments, enabling them to take control of their learning, and providing them with guidance and support to attain high standards. (Rosenthal & Jacobson, 1968).

5. Be aware of implicit biases: Creating a fair and inclusive learning environment that promotes academic achievement requires examining and challenging one's assumptions and beliefs about students, being open to different perspectives and experiences, and actively seeking opportunities to learn about students' diverse backgrounds. Educators aware of their implicit biases can take action to overcome them. (Lindsey et al., 2018).

These strategies represent the fundamental steps educators can take to avoid adding to the burdens shouldered by our students each day. While we may not always have the power to mitigate their struggles, we must strive to avoid exacerbating them. The circumstances within their homes and the systemic failures of education may lie beyond our control, but we can shape the experiences within our schools and classrooms. By focusing within our circle of influence, we can create an environment where our students feel supported and empowered to overcome the obstacles they face.

Build Positive Relationships

Establishing positive relationships with our students is essential for educators. Research has demonstrated that such connections can enhance student motivation, engagement, and academic achievement (Roorda et al., 2011). When our students perceive their educators as genuinely caring and supportive, they tend to be more driven to succeed and actively participate in the classroom. Those who feel connected to their educators exhibit greater school engagement, increased class participation, and fewer behavioral issues (Roorda et al., 2011). Reflect on the individuals you have worked hardest for—did you share a strong relationship with them? If not, your work ethic likely deteriorated over time.

The impact of teacher-student relationships on academic and social outcomes can be particularly significant for our students from historically marginalized groups. Research indicates that positive connections with educators can help counteract the adverse effects of poverty and foster academic success among marginalized students (Murray & Malmgren, 2005; Wentzel, 2016).

To cultivate positive relationships with our students, educators can employ a range of strategies, such as getting to know them, demonstrating genuine interest in their lives, being approachable and available, utilizing positive reinforcement, and incorporating humor (Berk, 2004; Hughes et al., 2001; Marzano et al., 2003; Skinner, 1965). These strategies demand no financial investment and can be implemented with relative ease. The only actual cost is time, but investing in nurturing relationships now will yield long-lasting positive effects and reduce time spent addressing issues later.

1. Educators must familiarize themselves with their backgrounds, interests, and learning styles to create a supportive learning environment and establish positive relationships with students. It is not appropriate or helpful to make assumptions about our students based solely on their race or ethnicity.

2. Building trust and rapport between educators and students is crucial to fostering genuine interest in students. This is accomplished by actively listening to their ideas and concerns, taking the time to engage with them, and creating a safe space where students can take academic risks without the fear of being judged. Many of our students are hesitant to make mistakes in front of others, which can impede their growth and hinder their willingness to learn.

3. An approachable and available educator can create a supportive learning environment and build positive relationships. Being approachable and available means educators are open to feedback and suggestions, promptly respond to students' emails or messages, and make time for individual conversations. Do not be afraid to ask students, "What can I do to support you?"

4. A positive classroom environment and positive relationships with students are fostered by positive reinforcement. Positive reinforcement involves acknowledging and celebrating our students' successes, providing incentives for good behavior or academic performance, and celebrating milestones and accomplishments. Celebrate students' efforts, and they will continue to push themselves through adversities.

5. Using humor to engage with students and make learning more engaging and enjoyable can also help to build positive relationships. Jokes, puns, and funny stories can create a positive classroom environment and promote student engagement. Asking silly

questions during attendance check-ins can bring humor to the classroom and allow us to learn about our students.

Fostering positive relationships with students is crucial for educators, as it can enhance motivation, engagement, and academic achievement. Students entangled in unfavorable relationships with educators may experience diminished motivation to learn and an increased likelihood of engaging in disruptive behaviors (Wentzel, 2016). Conversely, negative teacher-student relationships—marked by conflict and lack of trust—can detrimentally impact students' academic and social outcomes (Pekrun et al., 2017). As a teacher and an administrator, I have witnessed firsthand the profound influence of teacher-student relationships on students and their accomplishments. All educators can employ various strategies to cultivate positive connections, such as getting to know our students, demonstrating genuine interest in their lives, being approachable and available, using positive reinforcement, and incorporating humor. A later chapter will present a more in-depth exploration of positive student-teacher relationships.

Culturally Responsive Instructional Strategies

Educators should use culturally responsive instructional strategies to create an inclusive and supportive learning environment that is responsive to the diverse cultural backgrounds of their students (Ladson-Billings, 1995). Educators using culturally responsive instructional strategies can better connect with their students, support their learning, and promote positive academic outcomes (Gay, 2010). Creating inclusive environments must go beyond Black and Latino History Month or one-day celebrations like Indigenous People's Day and Holi celebrations.

Research has shown that students who perceive their school or classroom environments as unwelcoming or discriminatory may have lower academic achievement, lower self-esteem, and higher rates of behavior problems (Lee & Bowen, 2006; Solorzano et al., 2000). Furthermore, students who feel excluded from the learning community may disengage from school and may be less likely to participate in academic activities (Goodenow, 1993; Ryan & Deci, 2000a). Disengaged students can lead to lower academic motivation, lower attendance rates, and higher dropout rates (Eccles & Roeser, 2011; Portes & Rumbaut, 2014). Additionally, students who perceive their school or classroom environments as unwelcoming or discriminatory may experience psychological distress, such as anxiety, depression, and low self-worth (Denny & Lo, 2009; Romero & Roberts, 2003).

There are several ways that educators can use culturally responsive instructional strategies in classrooms. One approach is incorporating our students' cultural backgrounds and experiences into the curriculum. This can involve using culturally relevant materials, such as literature, music, and art, that reflect the diversity of students' experiences and perspectives (Nieto, 2010). For this to work requires educators to take the time to have conversations and research information about our students to really learn about them. Walking around the neighborhood and participating in community events can provide many insights into our students' lives.

Another strategy is engaging in culturally responsive instructional strategies, such as cooperative learning, where students work collaboratively in heterogeneous groups, and peer tutoring, where students with different skills and abilities work together to achieve a common goal (Gay, 2010). These strategies promote the development of cross-cultural communication skills. They can help our students learn from and appreciate one another's differences. Active facilitation is essential for this strategy's success. One cannot merely put our students in groups and expect optimal results without facilitating interactions. Everything we do requires intentionality.

Educators can also use culturally responsive instructional strategies to create a classroom environment that is culturally responsive and welcoming to all students. For example, educators can decorate the classroom or school with materials that reflect the diversity of their students, such as flags, posters, and maps. Having our students participate in decorating the school or classroom by making items or bringing in materials that represent them can increase engagement and ownership. Educators can also create a positive school and classroom culture by using positive affirmations and encouraging students to share their cultural experiences and perspectives (Gay, 2010).

Educators should use culturally responsive instructional strategies to create an inclusive and supportive learning environment that is responsive to the diverse cultural backgrounds of their students. To do so, they can incorporate students' cultural backgrounds and experiences into the curriculum, engage in culturally responsive instructional practices, and create a school and classroom environment that is culturally responsive and welcoming to all students.

Frequent and Constructive Feedback

Providing frequent and constructive feedback is essential to effective instruction that can enhance students' academic achievement (Hattie & Timperley, 2007). Feedback can help our students identify areas of strength and areas that need improvement. It can promote self-regulated learning by helping students monitor and adjust their learning strategies (Nicol & Macfarlane-Dick, 2006). Promoting self-regulated learning requires supporting our students in a world where they do not feel comfortable showing weakness. Our students love games and social media because they get instant feedback. They know how many people watched and liked their video. They know how many lives they have left and how much health the game's boss has. In both instances, they know their progress toward their goal.

Frequent and constructive feedback can be particularly beneficial for marginalized students. Research has shown that these students may be less likely to receive teacher feedback and may benefit from more feedback to improve their academic performance (Hattie & Timperley, 2007; Loeb & Reininger, 2004). Frequent feedback focused on the learning process rather than just the end result can help our students develop a growth mindset and a belief in their ability to improve (Dweck, 2006; Yeager & Dweck, 2012). This is particularly important for marginalized students, who may be more likely to hold fixed mindsets and view their intelligence as predetermined (Blackwellet al., 2007).

To provide frequent and constructive feedback, educators can use various strategies. One approach is to provide high-quality feedback on formative assessments, which are assessments that are designed to inform instruction and provide our students with information on their progress toward learning goals. Educators can use a variety of formative assessments, such as quizzes, exit tickets, and observations, to gather information about students' learning and provide targeted feedback on areas of strength and areas that need improvement (Black & Wiliam, 1998). Formative assessments must be intentional and aligned with goals. Formative assessments must go beyond marking questions right or wrong when possible.

Another strategy is to use descriptive feedback, which provides specific information to students about their performance and offers suggestions for improvement. Descriptive feedback should be timely, relevant, and clear, focusing on the task rather than the student (Hattie & Timperley, 2007). For example, rather than saying, "Good job!" or "You need to work harder," educators can provide feedback that is specific to the task, such as "Your essay is well-organized, but you need to include more evidence to support your arguments." Descriptive feedback not only informs students of areas of improvement but also shows our students that we care enough to take the time to look at what they did. Descriptive feedback does not mean that we are not allowed to praise effort. Praising effort is an essential part of building confidence and motivation in students. Descriptive feedback and praising effort both have their place.

To enhance student learning, educators can implement a feedback process that empowers students to reflect on their learning and set improvement goals. One effective strategy is to provide students with opportunities to self-assess their work, develop learning objectives, and monitor their progress over time. This approach effectively increases student engagement and academic achievement (Hattie & Timperley, 2007). Our students can and should give feedback to each other, which helps promote self-reflection and growth and improve the learning culture.

Providing frequent and constructive feedback is essential to effective instruction that can enhance students' academic achievement. This type of feedback can improve their motivation and engagement in learning, help them identify areas for improvement, and develop a growth mindset. To do so, educators should use formative assessments, provide specific descriptive feedback, and involve our students in the feedback process. Feedback is too crucial for it to be an afterthought if we want our student's academic achievement to improve.

High Expectations

Setting high expectations for all students is an essential aspect of effective teaching and learning that can positively impact student academic achievement (Rosenthal & Jacobson, 1968; Hattie, 2012). When educators have high expectations for their students, they create a culture of excellence and communicate to students that they believe in their potential to succeed (Fuligni et al., 2019). Unfortunately, research has shown that some educators hold low expectations for marginalized students (Lindsay & Hart, 2017; McKown & Weinstein, 2018). These low expectations can lead to disparities in academic achievement and exacerbate existing achievement gaps (Ferguson, 2019).

One study found that educators were more likely to view students of color as less capable and less motivated than White students, even with similar academic profiles (Gershenson et al., 2017). Another study showed that educators tend to overestimate the intellectual abilities of students from high socioeconomic backgrounds and underestimate the abilities of those from low socioeconomic backgrounds (Darling-Hammond et al., 2019).

To set high expectations for all students, educators can use various strategies. One approach is to provide clear and specific learning objectives for each lesson. There should be a balance between using language our students understand and aligning learning objectives with the standards. Educators should explain the lesson's purpose, the skills or knowledge that students will be expected to master, and the criteria for success (Tomlinson et al., 2003). Providing clear and specific learning objectives helps students understand their learning expectations and can motivate them to achieve them. It still surprises me when I speak to our students that many do not know the takeaway of the day's lesson. If students do not know what they are supposed to learn, they will not be able to connect to future and prior learning, which can hinder long-lasting and future learning. It is similar to driving without a destination. Sure, we will get somewhere, but is it where we should be?

Another strategy is to use challenging tasks and assignments that push students beyond their comfort zones. These tasks should be appropriately challenging and provide opportunities for students to develop their skills and knowledge (Hattie, 2012). The relationships we build with our students will determine how much we can challenge students and if pushing students out of their comfort zone will turn into a student putting a wall up. Our students will take up challenges and push themselves if they trust us. Educators can also provide opportunities for students to work collaboratively and support each other in achieving their goals. Developing a culture of learning and one where respect and rapport are a part of the environment will support collaborative work and support between students.

Educators can also use positive reinforcement to recognize and celebrate students' achievements. Positive reinforcement can include praising our students for their efforts and progress, recognizing their strengths, and encouraging them to continue to work toward their goals (Fuligni et al.,

2019). When students receive positive feedback and recognition for their efforts, they are likelier to continue to work hard and strive for excellence. While positive reinforcement is not a bad thing, it needs to evolve into students recognizing and celebrating their achievements on their own. When implementing positive reinforcement, one must ask themself, "How can I get our students to recognize their efforts and celebrate their achievements?" Extrinsic motivation can be great, but intrinsic motivation will lead to long-lasting success.

Setting high expectations for all students is an essential aspect of effective instruction that can positively impact academic achievement. To do so, educators can provide clear learning objectives, use challenging tasks and assignments, and provide opportunities for collaboration and positive reinforcement.

Implicit Biases

Educators should be aware of implicit biases to ensure they are not unintentionally perpetuating inequities in their classrooms (Ferguson, 2010). Implicit biases are attitudes or beliefs that operate outside of conscious awareness and can affect our behavior toward others (Devine et al., Cox, 2012). These biases can impact an educator's interactions with students, leading to differential treatment based on race, gender, or socioeconomic status (Okonofua et al., 2016). Implicit biases can also stem from an educator's past experiences with a student's family. Sometimes something as small as having a last name associated with negative experiences can lead to bias. There have been far too many times when I hear someone say, "Oh, I know that last name."

Implicit biases can affect how educators perceive and interact with our students, particularly those from marginalized groups. To become aware of implicit biases, educators can take several steps:

1. Educate themselves on implicit bias and how it can affect their interactions with students. Research has shown that learning about implicit bias can reduce its effects (Monteith et al., 2002).

2. Reflect on their own experiences and beliefs about students from different backgrounds. Reflecting should involve examining their assumptions, prejudices, and stereotypes and considering how they might affect their interactions with students.

3. Seek feedback from colleagues or other professionals. Educators can ask for feedback on their instructional practices and student interactions to identify areas where their biases may affect their behavior.

4. Engage in cultural competence training. Cultural competence training can help educators develop the skills and knowledge needed to interact effectively with students from diverse backgrounds (National Education Association, 2015).

5. Monitor their behavior and interactions with students. Educators can pay attention to their actions and words in the classroom or school to identify any biases affecting their interactions with students.

Educators can use several evidence-based strategies to reduce the impact of implicit biases toward marginalized students. One approach is engaging in intergroup contact, which promotes positive interactions between individuals from different social groups. Research has shown that intergroup contact can help reduce stereotypes and prejudice and promote positive attitudes and behaviors toward individuals from other social groups (Pettigrew & Tropp, 2006). Educators can facilitate intergroup contact by promoting diverse group work, creating opportunities for our students to engage with individuals from different backgrounds, and fostering a sense of community in the classroom.

Another evidence-based strategy is to use counter-stereotypic examples, which involve presenting examples that challenge existing stereotypes and biases. Research has shown that exposure to counter-stereotypic examples can help reduce the impact of implicit biases (Blair, 2002). Educators can use counter-stereotypic examples in their instruction by selecting materials and resources that challenge stereotypes and biases and by providing examples that highlight diverse experiences and perspectives within different social groups.

Awareness of implicit biases is vital for educators to create an equitable and inclusive learning environment for all students. Educators can recognize their biases through self-reflection, seeking feedback, and engaging in professional development. Self-reflection must occur regularly to identify and address any new or old biases they may hold, which can help create a more inclusive and equitable classroom environment. We can also use evidence-based strategies to reduce the impact of our biases on our instructional practices. By building strong relationships with our students, actively listening to their perspectives, and providing individualized support, educators can promote a more equitable and inclusive learning environment for all our students.

Am I willing to admit when I'm wrong or when my actions have contributed to the problem, and am I open to learning and growing from those mistakes?

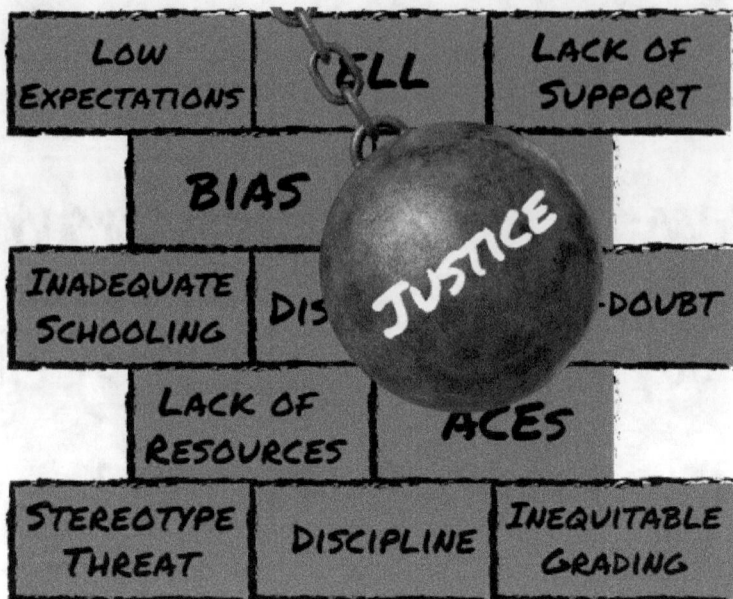

LOW EXPECTATIONS	...LL	LACK OF SUPPORT
BIAS		
INADEQUATE SCHOOLING	DIS	-DOUBT
LACK OF RESOURCES	ACES	
STEREOTYPE THREAT	DISCIPLINE	INEQUITABLE GRADING

JUSTICE

Chapter 3: Equality to Equity to Justice

Equality and Equity Are Not Enough.

Let me share a story of a young girl I knew from high school with you named Ana. Ana lived in a small two-bedroom apartment with her grandma and two younger siblings. Her grandma was her legal guardian and worked two jobs to make ends meet, leaving Ana to take care of her siblings most of the time. Ana wanted to be an engineer when she grew up and was excited to participate in our school's annual science fair.

Ana was passionate about science and had eagerly awaited the school's science fair for months. She spent countless hours researching and preparing her project in the school library during lunch. Ana was determined to participate even without access to the latest technology or resources that many of her classmates had. She knew winning the science fair would open up many opportunities for her.

On the science fair day, Ana arrived at school with her project in hand. However, she quickly realized she was at a disadvantage compared to her classmates. While some of her classmates had projects that were obviously made from purchased materials and likely had help from their parents, Ana's project was made from simple materials gathered from around her house. She used her little sister's dollar store paint set, cardboard from grocery store products that were found in the garbage, some leftover duct tape from a previous project, and some items she borrowed from neighbors and friends. She also used some of the resources the school provided to every student for the project.

Although everyone else's project was flashy, Ana was proud of hers and was very excited to present it to the judges. However, as the day went on, Ana noticed that many of her classmates' projects were given more attention and recognition than the project she made. Most people did not take the time to stop by her table to ask her about her project. Ana watched as her peers were praised for their projects while Her's was ignored.

Ana felt defeated and discouraged. She had worked so hard on her project, but she couldn't help feeling like she was being overlooked. Ana wondered whether having access to the same flashy resources as her classmates would have changed everyone's perception. After her bad experience at the science fair, she gave up on her dreams of being an engineer.

This story highlights the difference between equality and equity. In an equal system, everyone is given the same resources and opportunities. However, in Ana's case, this approach did not work as it often doesn't. Despite being given the same opportunity to participate in the science fair, Ana was disadvantaged compared to her classmates because of her socioeconomic status.

In an equitable system, students are provided resources and support based on their individual needs. This approach recognizes that not all students have the same opportunities and that some require more support to succeed. She could have had a fair chance to compete with her peers if Ana had been provided the needed resources and support.

Ana's story is gut-wrenching because it highlights the inequalities that many students face when trying to pursue their dreams. It is a reminder that access to resources and support can make all the difference in a student's success. We must work to level the playing field for all our students, regardless of their socioeconomic background.

Justice, equity, and equality are all important educational principles. Still, they represent different concepts with different educational policy and practice implications. People often confuse equality and equity as being the same thing, even though they are very different.

Equality in education refers to the principle of treating all students the same, regardless of their background or circumstances. Treating all students equally means giving them equal access to resources and opportunities, regardless of race, ethnicity, socioeconomic status, or other factors (Kozol, 2012). Equality does not consider any adversities our students face, including physical and learning disabilities or the fact that a student may be an English Language Learner. For a long time, most people thought that equality was all that was needed to close the achievement gap in education. Decades after the first measures were implemented, the achievement gap is getting larger, not smaller.

On the other hand, equity refers to the principle of providing every student with the resources and opportunities they need to succeed. It may involve different levels of support for different students based on their unique needs and circumstances (National Equity Project, 2019). Equity means addressing the root causes of educational disparities and providing targeted support to students from historically marginalized and underrepresented groups to ensure they have the same opportunities for success as their peers. Equitable practices have provided better success in closing the achievement gap, but much work still needs to be done.

Justice, as it relates to education, is focused on addressing systemic barriers and inequalities that have historically contributed to educational disparities and ensuring that every student has access to high-quality education (Ladson-Billings & Tate, 2006). Justice in education means working to dismantle structural barriers and systemic injustices that have perpetuated educational disparities and promoting policies and practices that promote equitable access to resources and opportunities for all students. Justice gets us closer to closing the achievement gap, but systematic changes are slow and often met with strong resistance.

In addition to addressing systemic issues, some scholars have proposed targeted interventions to address specific factors contributing to the achievement gap. For example, providing healthcare services in schools, increasing educator diversity, and implementing culturally responsive pedagogy have been suggested as potential strategies (Ladd, 2021; Noguera & Wing, 2016). While these measures will not fix all the systemic issues, these are areas that we can affect at the local levels.

Another approach is to focus on increasing opportunities for students from historically marginalized groups to develop and use their strengths and talents rather than solely focusing on deficits and remediation (Gay, 2010). This approach is grounded in the idea that our students from diverse backgrounds have unique perspectives and strengths that can be leveraged to promote academic achievement and success. This work must be intentional because looking for weaknesses, not strengths, is human nature.

46

Providing Healthcare Services in Schools

Providing healthcare services in schools for marginalized students can have numerous benefits. According to a study by Michael W. Beets and colleagues (2014), access to healthcare services in schools can help reduce health disparities among underserved populations, including marginalized students. The study found that providing comprehensive healthcare services in schools can improve access to preventive care, reduce missed school days, and improve overall health outcomes for our students.

One of the main benefits of providing healthcare services in schools is that it can improve access to care for underserved populations. Students from low-income families often lack access to primary healthcare, making it challenging to receive routine preventive care or treatment for chronic conditions (Garg et al., 2018). By providing healthcare services in schools, students can receive essential medical care, mental health services, and health education without missing school or traveling to a distant healthcare provider (Garg et al., 2018).

Another benefit of providing healthcare services in schools is that it can improve academic outcomes for our students. According to a report by the National Association of Community Health Centers (2013), students with access to healthcare services in schools are more likely to attend school regularly, have better academic performance, and are less likely to drop out of school due to health-related issues. While visits to health care providers are typically excused absences, our students still miss out on learning experiences when not in school. Most districts have policies allowing students to make up work. However, we can not necessarily make up the critical social interactions and teacher-guided learning that do not take place due to absences.

Despite the numerous benefits of providing healthcare services in schools, there are also several challenges associated with implementation. One of the main challenges is funding. According to a report by the National Conference of State Legislatures (2018), many school-based health centers struggle to secure adequate funding to provide comprehensive healthcare services to students. Amazingly, two essential services, healthcare, and education, which everyone should have equitable access to, are still challenging in many countries.

Another challenge is ensuring that students receive high-quality care from qualified healthcare providers. According to a study by the National Academy for State Health Policy (2019), many school-based health centers struggle to recruit and retain qualified healthcare providers due to low salaries and high turnover rates. Recruiting and retaining highly qualified providers requires significant investment in time and money, but its returns can be very fruitful. Partnerships with larger medical facilities and colleges can be beneficial in these cases.

Providing healthcare services in schools can have numerous benefits for marginalized students. However, implementation can be challenging due to funding and staffing issues. Addressing these challenges is critical to ensuring that all students have access to high-quality healthcare services that can improve their overall health outcomes and positively affect academic success.

Increasing Educator Diversity

Increasing educator diversity in schools is important for several reasons. Research has shown that students from diverse backgrounds benefit from having educators who share their cultural and ethnic backgrounds (Dee, 2004; Gershenson et al., 2017). Diverse educators can serve as role models and provide our students with a sense of belonging, which can improve their academic and social-emotional outcomes (Dee, 2004; Gershenson et al., 2017). In addition, educator diversity can promote cross-cultural understanding and help reduce prejudice and discrimination in schools (Gershenson et al., 2017).

The benefits of increasing educator diversity include the following:
1. Improved academic outcomes for students of color and those from low-income families (Dee, 2004).
2. Increased cultural competence among educators can help reduce classroom bias and discrimination (Tucker et al., 2019).
3. Improved educator retention rates, as educators from underrepresented groups are likelier to remain in schools serving diverse populations (Sutcher et al., 2016).

However, several challenges are associated with increasing educator diversity, including:

1. Limited diversity in the pool of educator candidates can make it challenging to recruit and retain educators from underrepresented groups (Bastian & Chen, 2016).
2. Educators need ongoing support and training to help them navigate the challenges of working in diverse schools (Tucker et al., 2019).
3. Systemic change is needed to address structural inequalities that discourage individuals from underrepresented groups from pursuing careers in education (Sutcher et al., 2016).

There are several strategies for increasing educator diversity in schools. One approach is to recruit and retain more educators from underrepresented groups (NCTQ, 2020). Creating targeted recruitment programs, offering financial incentives, and providing professional development opportunities that support the needs of diverse educators can help with recruitment and retention (NCTQ, 2020). Scholarships, grants, and loan forgiveness programs can help to make education a more attractive and accessible career choice for our students of color and those from low-income families (Sutcher et al., 2016). Another strategy is to provide support and mentoring for diverse educators to help them succeed and advance in their careers (NCTQ, 2020).

Improving educator preparation programs can also help increase educator diversity. Improved educator preparation programs should include incorporating diversity and cultural competency training into educator preparation programs and providing opportunities for pre-service educators to gain practical experience working with diverse students and communities (Darling-Hammond et al., 2017). Create alternative certification programs that provide a pathway for individuals from diverse backgrounds to become certified educators. These programs can provide additional support and training to help individuals overcome barriers to entry, such as the cost of educator certification exams (Bastian & Chen, 2016).

Addressing systemic and structural inequities contributing to educator shortages in high-needs schools and districts can also help increase educator diversity (Darling-Hammond et al., 2017). These inequities can be addressed by providing funding and resources to support educator recruitment and retention in high-needs areas and addressing low salaries and poor working conditions (Darling-Hammond et al., 2017).

There are several reasons why our students, especially students of color, may avoid the education profession due to negative and unwelcoming learning experiences. One of the main reasons is the lack of diversity and inclusivity in the education system. According to a report by the National Education Association (NEA), "the lack of diversity in the education workforce can lead to a lack of role models and mentors for students, particularly students of color, and a lack of understanding of cultural differences" (NEA, 2019).

Furthermore, students of color may have experienced discrimination, bias, and microaggressions in the classroom, which can create a negative perception of the education profession. A study by the Center for American Progress found that "students who experience bias in school are less likely to be interested in pursuing a career in education" (Center for American Progress, 2019). It all starts while they are students in school. Creating a school climate and culture that our students want to be in is important. Start recruiting diverse educators early by creating an environment for them as children that they want to return to as adults.

Marginalized students often avoid the education profession due to negative and unwelcoming learning experiences, lack of diversity and inclusivity in the education system, discrimination and bias, and systemic barriers. To encourage more marginalized to pursue a career in education, we must address these issues and create a more welcoming and inclusive environment for all students.

Implementing Culturally Responsive Pedagogy

Culturally responsive pedagogy (CRP) is an educational approach that emphasizes recognizing and valuing our students' diverse backgrounds, experiences, and perspectives. CRP can promote student engagement, academic achievement, and positive social-emotional outcomes (Gay, 2018; Ladson-Billings, 2019). CRP is nothing to be scared of. Despite ongoing rhetoric, CRP does not mean indoctrinating our students to believe the United States is bad and that all white people are racist.

There are several strategies for implementing culturally responsive pedagogy in the classroom. One approach is incorporating diverse perspectives and experiences into the curriculum and instructional materials (Ladson-Billings, 2019). Diverse perspectives can be included in the learning by selecting texts and other materials that reflect the diversity of students' backgrounds and experiences and incorporating examples and illustrations that highlight cultural and linguistic diversity. We should celebrate our differences instead of hiding from them or using them to divide us.

Another strategy is to create a classroom culture that values diversity and promotes inclusivity (Gay, 2018). Creating classroom norms and expectations that encourage respect and open-mindedness can create a culture that promotes inclusivity. Incorporating opportunities for student-led discussions and collaborative learning experiences that include different perspectives can create a culture that values diversity. Classroom culture determines how a student feels when they walk into the room. If a student feels alone and unwelcome, then they will be disengaged. No one wants to feel like they do not belong.

Building strong relationships with our students is also a key aspect of CRP. It may seem repetitive at this point, but positive teacher-student relationships and even positive student-student relationships are very important. This can be done by incorporating student voice and choice into the learning experience, providing opportunities for one-on-one conversations, and actively seeking to understand and connect with students' backgrounds and experiences (Ladson-Billings, 2019). Some of the challenges to implementing culturally responsive pedagogy include:

1. Lack of training and support: Many educators have not been trained in culturally responsive pedagogy and may not feel confident or comfortable implementing it in their classrooms. Additionally, schools may not have the necessary resources or support systems to help teachers incorporate CRP into their teaching.

According to a study by Ladson-Billings (2019), teachers need adequate training and support to effectively implement culturally responsive pedagogy in their classrooms. Without these resources, educators may struggle to create a culturally inclusive learning environment for our students.

2. Resistance to change: Some educators may resist changing their instructional practices and incorporating new approaches such as CRP. This resistance may be due to a lack of understanding or awareness of the benefits of CRP or a fear of losing control over the classroom.

Ladson-Billings (2019) noted that implementing CRP may require a shift in mindset and pedagogical practices. Educators who are resistant to change may require additional support and resources to help them feel more comfortable with CRP. Often, change is difficult when we think we will not get support.

3. Limited resources: Schools with limited resources may struggle to implement CRP effectively. Limited resources include a lack of funds to purchase culturally relevant materials or technology or a lack of time to dedicate to professional development for staff.

According to a study by Milner and Howard (2018), schools with limited resources may struggle to implement CRP meaningfully. Without adequate resources, educators may be unable to create a culturally responsive learning environment for our students.

4. Inadequate assessment and evaluation: There may be a lack of tools and strategies for assessing and evaluating the effectiveness of CRP in the classroom. Without proper assessment and evaluation, it may be challenging to determine the impact of CRP on student learning and achievement.

As Ladson-Billings (2019) noted, it is crucial to have a systematic approach to assessing and evaluating the effectiveness of CRP. This approach may include using various assessment tools, such as student surveys or classroom observations, to gather data on the impact of CRP on student learning.

Ongoing professional development and self-reflection are essential for implementing CRP effectively (Gay, 2018). Educators can engage in professional development opportunities that focus on cultural competency, equity, and inclusivity, reflect on their biases and assumptions, and seek opportunities to learn from and connect with our students and families from diverse backgrounds. If we ask eight different people what culturally responsive pedagogy or cultural competency is, we are likely to get different answers. Professional development is vital to ensure a common language and equitable approach.

Focus on Strengths and Talents.

Focusing on the strengths and talents of marginalized students is crucial for their academic and personal success. Historically, these students have been marginalized and subjected to negative stereotypes and biases that hinder their growth and development. While it is essential to identify and address areas of weakness or challenge, a strengths-based approach can help our students build on their existing skills and assets rather than solely focusing on deficits and remediation (Elias & Langer, 2017). By shifting the focus from deficits to strengths, educators can create a positive and supportive learning environment that empowers students and enhances their academic performance. This approach's numerous benefits include improved self-esteem, motivation, and academic achievement (Kim & Bayne, 2019).

One of the main benefits of focusing on students' strengths and talents is its positive impact on their self-esteem. When our students feel valued and appreciated for their abilities, they are more likely to develop a positive self-concept and a growth mindset. Our students' positive self-concept and growth mindset lead to greater motivation and engagement in learning, resulting in improved academic achievement (Molina & Starr, 2020). Focusing on strengths and talents also helps create a more inclusive learning environment that promotes diversity and celebrates all students' unique backgrounds and experiences.

If part of our purpose is to help our students be independent contributors to society, we must give them more control over their learning. Several strategies exist for developing and using students' strengths and talents in the classroom. One approach is incorporating opportunities for student choice and autonomy into the learning experience. Incorporating choice and autonomy can be done by providing opportunities for our students to choose topics or projects that align with their interests and strengths and by incorporating opportunities for student-led learning and collaboration (Linley & Harrington, 2006).

Another strategy is to use assessments and feedback that focus on student strengths and progress rather than solely on areas of challenge or deficit (Elias & Langer, 2017). Educators can provide feedback acknowledging and building on our students' strengths and use assessments focusing on progress and growth rather than just outcomes. This strategy can help our students shift from a fixed mindset into a growth mindset.

Despite the many benefits of focusing on strengths, some challenges must be addressed. One of the biggest challenges is the prevalence of negative stereotypes and biases within society and the education system. These biases can manifest in low expectations, tracking, and cultural misunderstandings, hindering students' academic and personal growth (Kim & Bayne, 2019). Additionally, educators may struggle with identifying and nurturing students' strengths, especially if they have been trained to focus on deficits rather than assets.

Another challenge is the lack of resources and support for a strengths-based approach. This may include educator training, resources for identifying and nurturing our students' strengths, and support from school administrators and policymakers (Molina & Starr, 2020). Additionally, there may be resistance to change from educators, parents, and students who are accustomed to a deficit-based approach to education.

Ongoing professional development and self-reflection can help educators adopt a strengths-based approach. Educators can engage in professional development opportunities that focus on strengths-based practices and self-reflection and seek feedback and support from colleagues, families, and students to help them better understand and build on student strengths and assets (Elias & Langer, 2017).

Justice Contributions: Critical Self-Reflection

Educators can contribute to justice in education by engaging in critical self-reflection and ongoing inquiry into their beliefs and practices and actively seeking out opportunities to promote equity and inclusivity in their classrooms and schools (Ladson-Billings & Tate, 2006a). To determine whether they are contributing to justice in education, educators may consider the following questions:

1. Am I providing all students with high-quality learning opportunities and resources, regardless of their background or circumstances?
2. Am I working to address and dismantle systemic barriers and inequalities contributing to educational disparities?
3. Am I using culturally responsive instructional strategies that recognize and value my students' diverse backgrounds and experiences?
4. Am I creating a safe and inclusive learning environment that promotes all students' academic and social-emotional growth?
5. Am I engaging in ongoing professional development and seeking opportunities to deepen my understanding of equity and social justice issues in education?

In their self-reflection, educators may find that there are things that they can directly control or influence and those they cannot. By asking themselves these questions and engaging in ongoing reflection and inquiry, educators can take concrete steps to promote justice and equity in education and ensure that they contribute to all students' success. It isn't easy to put into one book all the different outcomes that come from this process, but there are various common steps educators can take to promote justice and equity in education.

One approach is seeking out specific professional development or learning opportunities that meet the areas of growth determined from the self-reflection related to cultural competence, diversity, equity, and inclusion (CDEI) (Ginwright, 2018). Educators can also seek diverse perspectives and actively listen to students, families, and community members to understand their experiences, needs, and perspectives (Lindsey et al., 2018).

Another step educators can take is to examine and critically reflect on their own biases and assumptions, and work to develop culturally responsive instructional practices that recognize and affirm our students' diverse backgrounds, experiences, and identities (Hammond, 2015). This includes creating an inclusive and welcoming learning environment for all students and providing opportunities for them to explore and express their identities and cultures (Lindsey et al., 2018).

In addition, educators can work to address systemic barriers and inequalities within the education system by advocating for policies and practices that promote equity and social justice (Ginwright, 2018). Addressing systemic barriers and inequalities involves working with other educators, administrators, policymakers, and community members to address school funding, access to resources, and disciplinary policies that disproportionately impact marginalized students (Lindsey et al., 2018). Many issues need to be addressed, and many more cannot be addressed alone, but it only takes one person to start a conversation that can lead to the changes our students need.

Another step educators can take is to intentionally incorporate social justice themes and issues into the curriculum, providing opportunities for students to critically examine and address societal issues related to power, privilege, and oppression (Hammond, 2015). Service-learning projects and advocacy efforts that promote equity and justice in their communities and beyond are great ways to engage students in these issues (Lindsey et al., 2018).

Finally, educators can collaborate with families and community members to create partnerships and support systems that promote student success and well-being. This includes engaging in ongoing communication and collaboration with families to understand their needs and perspectives and working to create a supportive school climate that values and respects the cultural and linguistic diversity of all students (Ginwright, 2018). Collaboration is the key to dismantling systemic barriers and inequalities effectively. Alone one person can make ripples, but together we can make waves.

In the pursuit of justice in education, we must ensure that every voice is heard, every talent is nurtured, and every potential is realized.

Chapter 4: A World of Instant Gratification

Alex, a 16-year-old boy who lived in a poor neighborhood of a small town, was a top-performing student until grade 8. His academic achievement significantly reduced during his first two years of high school. Alex told me that he attributed this deficit to feeling lost and alone. At the time, He felt like no one cared about him or his future. He felt like he was stuck in a rut, and his grades reflected it.

Alex's family was too busy working multiple jobs to make ends meet, and they didn't have much time to help him with his studies or the encouraging words he needed. There were days when he had no interactions with adults other than those at his school. Many of his friends from middle school moved on to local regional and specialty high schools seeking career learning he was not interested in. He tried to make new friends but found that most were more interested in social media and video games than studying. Alex began to feel like nobody understood him or what he was going through, or at the very least, cared enough to find out.

Feeling disconnected and unfulfilled, Alex turned to social media and other online platforms for comfort. He became addicted to likes, comments, followers, and false perceptions of real life that were put out into the world. He often succumbed to the rabbit hole of videos found on the various internet platforms. Social media soon fulfilled his loneliness and gave him a false sense of belonging. He felt as though he had a purpose, even though he was not doing well in school.

In his junior year of High School, Alex got a new substitute teacher for math while his teacher was out on medical leave named Coach Allen. Coach Allen was Alex's old basketball coach from when he played in the city recreation league during middle school. Even though it had been a few years since they had seen each other, Coach Allen remembered Alex and was excited to reconnect with him.

Coach Allen noticed Alex was struggling and offered to help him get back on track. He started by building a relationship with Alex and getting to know him as a person, not just as a student. Their shared love of basketball provided a natural connection point for them, and Coach Allen used their shared interest to help motivate Alex academically.

Coach Allen used a variety of strategies to motivate Alex, including setting realistic goals, providing positive feedback, and offering support and encouragement. He also helped Alex see that he had a greater worth and purpose beyond social media and that his education was critical to achieving his dreams. Even after his assignment to Alex's math class had ended, he continued to check in with Alex and work with him.

Through hard work and perseverance, Alex began to see improvements in his grades. He was more focused and motivated and felt like he had a purpose again. Coach Allen's support and guidance helped him realize that his future was bright and that he could achieve great things.

Coach Allen used their shared interest in basketball to build trust and help Alex feel comfortable opening up to him about his struggles. He leveraged their relationship to help motivate Alex academically. Through their mentorship relationship, Coach Allen helped Alex rediscover his passion for learning and his sense of purpose.

In the end, Alex learned that true fulfillment comes from hard work and dedication, not instant gratification on social media, which gave him a false sense of approval. He discovered that he had a greater worth and purpose than ever imagined and that his education was the key to unlocking his full potential. Thanks to Coach Allen's help, Alex turned his life around, achieved success in school, and graduated on time. Alex is now in a four-year university where he is majoring in Computer Science with a concentration in Cyber Security. Alex also participates in a local mentoring program in hopes of helping students like him.

Do I Understand the World My Students Are Living In?

Growing up in the 21st century has been shaped by rapid technological advancements, changes in cultural attitudes, and global events such as the COVID-19 pandemic. This has led to notable differences in the experiences of children and adolescents compared to those who grew up 10 or 20 years ago.

One significant change in the past decade has been the increasing use of technology, particularly social media, among young people. Research shows that social media use is associated with positive and negative outcomes, including increased social connectedness and exposure to cyberbullying (Best et al., 2014). Additionally, the prevalence of smartphones and the internet has enabled young people to access information and connect with others in ways that were not possible 10 or 20 years ago.

The COVID-19 pandemic has also had a significant impact on the experiences of young people. School closures and remote learning have disrupted traditional modes of education and socialization (Lee, 2020). The pandemic's toll on mental health has been especially challenging for young people experiencing increased anxiety and depression (Golberstein et al., 2021).

Cultural attitudes towards gender, sexuality, and racial justice have also shifted in the past 10 to 20 years. Young people today are growing up in an environment where conversations about social justice and equity are more common and accepted than in the past. For example, recent years have seen increased activism among young people around issues such as climate change and gun control (Bloom, 2019).

Growing up in the 21st century has been shaped by technological advancements, the COVID-19 pandemic, and shifting cultural attitudes. These factors have resulted in notable differences in the experiences of children and adolescents compared to those who grew up 10 or 20 years ago. The world our students are living in today is not the world we lived in when we were kids. Suggesting so to our students or using that in our comparisons creates a bias and disconnect that can hinder our ability to serve our students to our full potential.

Instant Gratification

In today's society, students have access to various forms of technology, such as smartphones and social media, which can provide instant gratification and distraction from academic work. Instant gratification, which refers to the desire for immediate rewards or results, has become more prevalent in today's society, particularly with the widespread use of technology. This has raised concerns about its potential impact on student motivation and academic achievement.

Research has found that instant gratification can negatively affect student motivation and academic achievement. For example, a study by Rosen et al. (2013) found that using social media and other technology is associated with lower academic performance among students. The researchers suggest that this may be due to the distracting nature of these technologies, which can lead to decreased attention and reduced learning.

Similarly, a study by Tice and Bratslavsky (2000) found that the desire for instant gratification can reduce students' motivation to persist in challenging tasks. They found that when students were presented with an easy task with an immediate reward, they were less likely to persist in a subsequent difficult task that did not offer an immediate reward.

Moreover, a study by Vohs et al. (2013) found that mere exposure to cues associated with instant gratification, such as images of fast food or money, can reduce students' persistence and performance on academic tasks. The researchers suggest that this effect may be due to the activation of reward-seeking behavior incompatible with the effort required for academic achievement.

Research has shown that marginalized students are more likely to spend time on social media, which can negatively impact their academic achievement (Manca & Ranieri, 2016). Additionally, our students of color may face unique challenges related to access to technology, including disparities in internet access and computer ownership (Warschauer & Matuchniak, 2010). Lack of internet access and computer ownership can further exacerbate the adverse effects of instant gratification on academic achievement.

Furthermore, instant gratification can have a more significant impact on student motivation for marginalized students. Marginalized students may be more likely to prioritize immediate rewards, such as entertainment and socialization, over long-term goals, such as academic success and career aspirations (Tangney et al., 2004). This can lead to decreased motivation to engage in academic work and increased feelings of boredom or apathy toward learning.

Research suggests that instant gratification can have a negative impact on student motivation and academic achievement. The distracting nature of technology, the desire for immediate rewards, and exposure to cues associated with instant gratification can all reduce students' persistence and performance on academic tasks. Add this to the challenges our marginalized students already face, and we can see why we need a systematic approach if we ever want to reduce or close the achievement gap.

Mitigating Instant Gratification

The concept of instant gratification, or the desire for immediate reward, negatively impacts our students' motivation and academic achievement. Addressing student motivation and academic achievement in the context of instant gratification can be challenging. One significant challenge is the widespread use of technology and social media, which can be highly distracting and lead to reduced attention and learning (Rosen et al., 2013). Additionally, the desire for immediate rewards and the exposure to cues associated with instant gratification can reduce students' persistence and performance on academic tasks (Tice & Bratslavsky, 2000; Vohs et al., 2013).

Another challenge is the potential impact of instant gratification on students from historically marginalized communities. Research has found that these students are more likely to experience academic motivation and achievement challenges, including a lack of access to resources and support (National Center for Education Statistics, 2021). Moreover, the effects of instant gratification may be compounded for these students, as they may have fewer opportunities to engage in activities that promote academic motivation and achievement. However, there are several strategies that educators can use to address this issue.

Research has found that instant gratification can reduce students' motivation to persist in challenging tasks (Tice & Bratslavsky, 2000). One strategy for addressing this is to provide our students with a sense of progress and accomplishment through feedback and recognition (Hattie & Timperley, 2007). This can help to counteract the effects of instant gratification by providing students with a sense of achievement that is more immediate and tangible than the long-term rewards of academic success. Praising effort and celebrating small wins can go a long way for our students' craving confirmation of their abilities.

Building intrinsic motivation is not only long-lasting, but it is a major mechanism in overcoming the addiction to extrinsic motivations from others. By encouraging students to take an active role in their learning, educators can help foster a sense of autonomy and motivation that is less susceptible to instant gratification. Another strategy is promoting self-regulated learning, which involves teaching students how to set goals, monitor their progress, and adjust their learning strategies based on their performance (Zimmerman, 2002).

Often our students gravitate toward negative situations, whether it is gangs, substance abuse, social media, or other things, in their search for a sense of belonging and being part of something bigger than themselves. Moreover, educators can help mitigate the negative effects of instant gratification by creating a classroom environment conducive to learning. This may involve minimizing distractions, such as reducing technology use during class time and creating a positive and supportive learning climate (Pekrun & Linnenbrink-Garcia, 2014).

Instant gratification can have a negative impact on student motivation and academic achievement. Still, educators can take steps to address this issue. Providing feedback and recognition, promoting self-regulated learning, and creating a positive learning environment are all strategies that can help mitigate instant gratification's adverse effects. Particularly for students from historically marginalized communities, addressing student motivation and academic achievement in the context of instant gratification can be challenging. However, by providing our students with resources and support and addressing systemic barriers, we can help all students develop the skills and habits needed to succeed academically.

Motivation is the Driver.

Motivation theory refers to frameworks describing how and why people behave in specific ways, particularly concerning achieving goals or satisfying needs. One of the most prominent motivation theories is self-determination theory (SDT), which describes how people are motivated by fulfilling basic psychological needs (Ryan & Deci, 2017b). According to SDT, individuals have three basic psychological needs: autonomy, competence, and relatedness. Autonomy refers to the need for self-determination and choice, competence refers to the need for mastery and growth, and relatedness refers to the need for social connection and belonging.

Another prominent motivation theory is the goal-setting theory, which describes how setting specific and challenging goals can lead to higher performance and motivation levels (Locke & Latham, 2019). Goal-setting theory suggests that goals serve as a reference point for individuals, providing direction and focus for their actions.

Expectancy theory is another well-known motivation theory that emphasizes the role of perceived effort-to-performance relationships and performance-to-outcome relationships in shaping motivation (Vroom, 1964). According to expectancy theory, individuals are motivated to engage in activities that they believe will lead to desired outcomes. This motivation is influenced by their expectations about the likelihood and value of those outcomes.

One factor that has been shown to affect student motivation negatively is anxiety. Research has found that anxiety can undermine students' self-efficacy and control, leading to lower motivation and poorer academic performance (Pekrun et al., 2017). Another factor is stress, which can lead to feelings of burnout and fatigue, reducing our students' motivation and engagement.

Moreover, other factors that can negatively affect motivation in students include a lack of interest in the material, low self-esteem, lack of self-regulation skills, and a lack of perceived relevance of the material (Järvelä et al., 2016). Additionally, negative academic experiences, such as low grades or negative feedback, can diminish students' motivation to engage in academic tasks (Eccles & Wigfield, 2002).

Several interventions have been suggested to address these adverse effects on student motivation. For example, providing students more autonomy, choice, and control over their learning has increased motivation and engagement (Reeve, 2012). Additionally, fostering positive emotions such as interest and enjoyment of the material has increased motivation and academic performance (Pekrun et al., 2007). Finally, promoting a growth mindset, or the belief that abilities can be developed through effort and learning, has increased student motivation and resilience in the face of academic challenges (Yeager & Dweck, 2012).

Principal Baruti Kafele has described the "attitude gap" as a significant barrier to student success that can undermine even the best efforts of educators. The attitude gap refers to the disparity between students who are motivated and engaged in their learning and those who are not (Kafele, 2013).

In motivation theory, the attitude gap can be understood as a manifestation of the differences in student motivation and engagement central to many motivational theories. For example, the Self-Determination Theory (SDT) emphasizes the importance of intrinsic motivation, or the drive to engage in activities for their inherent rewards, as a critical factor in student success (Ryan & Deci, 2000b). Our students lacking intrinsic motivation may be less likely to put forth the effort or persist in facing challenges, leading to poor academic performance and disengagement from school.

Similarly, the Expectancy-Value Theory (EVT) emphasizes the importance of both expectancy beliefs (the belief that one can complete a task) and task value (the degree to which a task is perceived as important or relevant) in driving student motivation and engagement (Eccles & Wigfield, 2002). Students who lack positive expectancy beliefs or perceive a task as low in value may be less motivated to engage in the task or may give up more easily when faced with challenges.

Addressing the attitude gap requires a concerted effort to understand and address the underlying factors contributing to our student motivation and engagement. This may involve providing students with opportunities to engage in personally meaningful and relevant activities, promoting a growth mindset emphasizing the potential for learning and growth, and providing targeted support and resources to struggling students (Kafele, 2013).

Unique Motivation Challenges

Motivation is a critical factor in student success and is particularly important for marginalized students. Marginalized students face additional unique challenges impacting their motivation and academic achievement. Research has identified several factors that can contribute to these challenges, including stereotype threat, cultural mismatch, and the achievement gap (Owens & Lynch, 2012).

Stereotype threat, as discussed in Chapter 1, refers to the experience of anxiety or concern about confirming negative stereotypes about one's racial or ethnic group (Steele & Aronson, 1995). One mechanism by which stereotype threat affects motivation is through its impact on self-efficacy or one's belief in one's ability to perform a task successfully (Hoyt & Blascovich, 2010). When our students experience stereotype threat, they may doubt their ability to succeed and become less motivated to engage in the task. They perceive it as an opportunity to confirm the negative stereotype about their group. This can lead to a self-fulfilling prophecy, where the fear of confirming the stereotype leads to poorer performance (Steele & Aronson, 1995).

Stereotype threat can also undermine student motivation by reducing the relevance and value of academic tasks to students' identities and goals (Cohen & Garcia, 2008). Students who perceive that academic tasks are irrelevant to their lives or goals are less likely to engage with them and invest effort in their completion.

Cultural mismatch refers to the discrepancy between our students' cultural backgrounds and experiences and the norms and expectations of schools and educational systems (Ogbu, 1992; Mendoza & Reese, 2018). Cultural mismatch occurs when the values and norms of a student's home culture are not aligned with those of the school culture (Suarez-Orozco et al., 2010). This misalignment can lead to feelings of disconnection and disengagement from school, which can, in turn, impact motivation and academic achievement.

Ogbu (1992) posited that cultural mismatch occurs when schools and educational systems fail to recognize and respond to the cultural diversity of their students and instead impose dominant cultural norms and expectations that may not align with students' cultural values and experiences. Mendoza and Reese (2018) argue that cultural mismatch can also arise from the intersection of multiple cultural identities and experiences, such as race, ethnicity, gender, and socioeconomic status.

The achievement gap, which refers to persistent disparities in academic performance between our students from different racial and socioeconomic backgrounds, can also contribute to challenges in motivation and achievement for marginalized students (Reardon, 2011). Our students who are constantly reminded of the achievement gap may experience a sense of hopelessness or lack of self-efficacy, which can negatively impact their motivation to succeed.

One challenge marginalized students face is a sense of alienation and disconnection from academic environments. For example, research has shown that students of color often feel excluded from mainstream academic culture, leading to disengagement and low motivation (Ogbu, 1992). Similarly, marginalized students may feel that academic settings are not designed for their success and may disengage from academic pursuits (Purdie-Vaughns & Eibach, 2008).

Creating academic environments that are inclusive, culturally responsive, and supportive of all students can go a long way. To support the motivation of marginalized students, it is essential to develop interventions that address these groups' unique challenges and strengths. For example, interventions that promote a sense of belonging, such as mentorship programs and academic support services, can help to address feelings of disconnection and exclusion. Similarly, interventions that challenge negative stereotypes and bias, such as stereotype intervention programs, can help to promote a sense of confidence and self-efficacy in academic pursuits (Cohen & Garcia, 2008). Additionally, interventions that promote a growth mindset, or the belief that academic abilities can be developed through effort and learning, may be particularly effective for these groups (Yeager & Dweck, 2012).

Addressing the challenges that marginalized students face in terms of motivation requires understanding the complex social and cultural factors that influence motivation and engagement in these populations. A growing body of research suggests that factors such as stereotypes, discrimination, and poverty can negatively impact student motivation and achievement (Cokley et al., 2018; Steele, 2010). It is also essential to recognize and challenge the structural barriers contributing to educational inequity, such as funding disparities, unequal access to resources, and discriminatory policies and practices (Steele, 2010). Advocating for policies that promote educational equity and creating more just and equitable school systems can help address these underlying factors and promote student motivation and engagement.

The RoI of Learning

A student's perceived Return on Investment (RoI) of learning is essential to student success, particularly for marginalized students. Addressing the RoI of learning involves ensuring that students see the value and relevance of their education and have the skills and resources necessary to translate their learning into real-world opportunities. RoI of Learning focuses on building the intrinsic motivation of students. Intrinsic motivation is a critical factor in fostering lifelong learners. It is driven by a deep interest and enjoyment in learning for their own sake rather than external rewards or pressures (Ryan & Deci, 2000b).

Students live in a world of instant gratification; the best way to combat that is by adding long-term value. One approach to addressing the RoI of learning is career-focused education and experiential learning opportunities. For example, internships, apprenticeships, and other work-based learning experiences can help students to see the connections between their education and future career opportunities. These experiences can also provide students with the practical skills and knowledge necessary to succeed in the workforce, regardless of their background or socioeconomic status. When we can show students the value of their learning now, and they can see the long-term value, we begin to build the intrinsic motivation needed to fuel the lifelong learner.

Another approach to addressing the RoI of learning is using culturally responsive pedagogy, which involves incorporating students' cultural backgrounds and experiences into the curriculum (Ladson-Billings, 1995). By doing so, educators can help to make learning more relevant and engaging for marginalized students. This approach can also help to challenge negative stereotypes and biases that may undermine student motivation and achievement (Ladson-Billings, 2019). When the learning is irrelevant or disengaging, we add to the learning cost and reduce the short-term and long-term value.

Furthermore, addressing the RoI of learning also requires focusing on equity and access to educational resources. For example, ensuring that students have access to quality educational materials, such as textbooks and technology, can help to support their learning and improve their academic outcomes (Reardon & Portilla, 2016). Additionally, providing students access to academic support services, such as tutoring and mentorship programs, can help address learning barriers and promote student success (Santa-Ramirez, 2022). The emotional value that comes from seeing others invest in us is often overlooked, but when we put deep thought into it, we will understand how it all contributes to a positive culture and climate. As it has been said by hundreds of people before me, the grass is greener where we water it.

It is vital to increase the ROI (return on investment) of learning for marginalized students because education is a powerful tool for promoting social mobility and reducing inequities. However, students from these groups often face significant barriers to accessing high-quality educational opportunities and achieving academic success. By increasing the ROI of learning, educators can help to maximize the impact of educational investments and ensure that our students from all backgrounds have the skills and knowledge they need to succeed in school and life. This requires creating an engaging, challenging, and supportive learning environment that recognizes and values each student's strengths and experiences. Ultimately, increasing the ROI of learning is essential for promoting equity and social justice in our society.

Do I acknowledge the impact of instant gratification on students' learning styles and adapt my teaching methods accordingly?

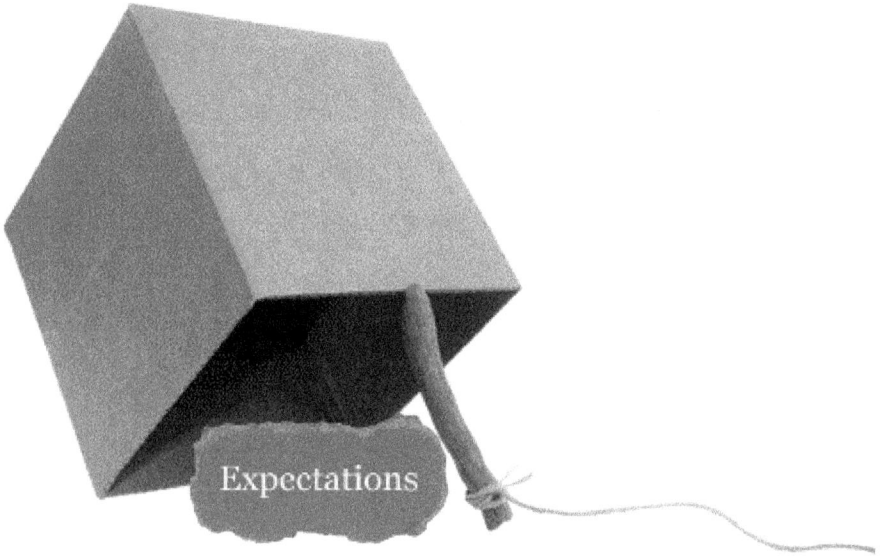

Chapter 5: The High Expectations Trap

Miguel was a bright and curious teenager when he came to the United States of America. His family had recently immigrated to the small, densely populated town. Miguel was still adjusting to his new environment and struggled to learn English. At school, Miguel's teachers noticed his difficulties with the English language but were poorly trained on how to support him. Instead of encouraging him to reach his full potential, they set low expectations for him. He did not feel as though any of his teachers thought that he would excel academically because of his language barrier and the lack of formal education that he received from his home country.

Miguel's days were filled with frustration and disappointment as he struggled to find his place. He felt trapped by his teachers' low expectations and started internalizing these beliefs. He began to think that he would never succeed, no matter how hard he tried. Miguel also felt alone and out of place with other students who seemed to pick up the English language faster than him. As a result, Miguel's performance and behavior in school started to decline.

One day, while Miguel wandered the hallways during lunch, he stumbled upon the school's library. The librarian, Ms. Sanchez, noticed him and greeted him with a warm smile. She could see the curiosity in Miguel's eyes as he gazed at the books lining the shelves. Sensing that something was up and he probably needed a friend, Ms. Sanchez spoke with him and encouraged him to explore the library.

Over time, Miguel began to spend more and more time in the library, forming a close bond with Ms. Sanchez. She recognized the potential many had failed to see and was determined to help him break through the barriers holding him back. Ms. Sanchez taught Miguel that he did not have to accept the limitations set for him by others. She shared her story with him and helped him believe he could achieve anything he wanted.

Ms. Sanchez started by offering Miguel books in his native language, allowing him to enjoy the wonders of literature without the frustration of a language barrier. She also brought some resources from home to supplement the school's library offerings. Gradually, Ms. Sanchez introduced him to English books, carefully selecting stories to capture his interest and help him improve his language skills. She worked with him patiently, helping him decipher new words and phrases and encouraging him to practice speaking English.

As Miguel's language skills improved, so did his confidence. He began to participate more actively in class, no longer feeling held back by the expectations of his teachers. With the support of Ms. Sanchez, Miguel learned that he could reach new heights and did not have to settle for the limitations imposed upon him.

Miguel's transformation did not go unnoticed. His teachers realized the error in their assumptions and started to set higher expectations for him. As Miguel continued to excel academically and grew confident, his peers also started to view him with admiration and respect. Miguel had become a shining example of what can be achieved when a student is supported and allowed to break free from the constraints placed upon them.

All it took was the belief and dedication of a kind-hearted school librarian who refused to let a young boy be held back by barriers placed on him by others. Ms. Sanchez's unwavering support and guidance helped Miguel discover his true potential and taught him that the only limits that genuinely exist are the ones we impose upon ourselves. Thus, Miguel soared to new heights, forever grateful for the librarian who believed in him when no one else did.

The High Expectations Trap: A Phenomenon

High expectations refer to the belief that one or others can perform at a superior level, achieving more significant outcomes or adhering to higher standards (Burnette et al., 2013). High expectations can have benefits and pitfalls, influencing various personal and interpersonal life aspects.

Benefits of High Expectations:
- Enhanced performance: High expectations can increase motivation and a stronger drive to achieve the desired goals. Research has shown that when individuals believe they can achieve a goal, they are more likely to put in the effort and persist in facing challenges (Dweck, 2015).
- Increased self-efficacy: People with high expectations often have a more heightened sense of self-efficacy or the belief in their ability to accomplish a task (Bandura, 1977). This sense of self-efficacy can contribute to increased motivation, perseverance, and resilience when faced with obstacles.
- Improved relationships: In interpersonal contexts, having high expectations for others can lead to the Pygmalion effect, where people live up to the expectations placed upon them (Rosenthal & Jacobson, 1968). When individuals perceive that others hold them in high regard, they may feel more motivated to meet those

expectations, ultimately leading to better performance and stronger relationships.

Pitfalls of High Expectations:

- Unrealistic expectations: High expectations can become problematic if they are not grounded in reality. Setting unattainable goals can lead to frustration, decreased motivation, and a sense of failure (Locke & Latham, 2002).

- Increased stress and anxiety: Consistently striving to meet high expectations can result in increased stress and anxiety, especially when individuals are unable to achieve the desired outcomes (Neff & Vonk, 2009). Over time, this can contribute to burnout and other negative mental health consequences.

- Strained relationships: High expectations can strain relationships if perceived as unreasonable or unattainable. This can lead to resentment and feelings of inadequacy, ultimately damaging the quality of the relationship (Rusbult et al., 1998).

High expectations can lead to numerous benefits, such as increased motivation, self-efficacy, and improved relationships. However, it is essential to be mindful of the potential pitfalls, including unrealistic expectations, increased stress, and strained relationships. Balancing high expectations with a realistic understanding of one's capabilities and limitations can help maximize the benefits while minimizing the potential drawbacks. In the most successful video games, there is a balance between difficulty and progress. It has to be challenging enough to want to conquer it, but it has to be reachable, even with bonus items or power-ups to help us keep progressing. If we are stuck on the same level for a long time or get through all the levels too easily, we are not as likely to finish the game over a well-balanced one.

The "high expectations trap" is a phenomenon where individuals set unrealistic and unattainable goals for themselves, leading to a cycle of self-doubt, stress, and burnout. This trap is often seen in high achievers who have a history of success and are driven to maintain their level of excellence. However, when these individuals set unrealistic expectations, they may struggle to meet them, leading to negative self-talk, anxiety, and depression. Outside influences, including family, friends, educators, and other mentors, can spur these unrealistic and unattainable goals.

One major factor that contributes to the high expectations trap is social comparison. When individuals or those with influence over them compare them to others achieving at a high level, they may feel pressure to match or exceed that level of success. This can lead to setting too high and unrealistic goals for their current abilities, leading to disappointment and feelings of failure when they cannot meet them. Setting realistic goals does not mean that an individual will not or cannot exceed those goals. I aimed to reach at least 100 pages when writing this book, but that was my glass ceiling. I knew that I would give my very best and push myself. If 100 pages were all I wrote, I was okay with that, but if I could go beyond that goal, I would not stop.

In today's age of social media, students are falling into this trap more than ever. Social media has masked what success is by putting out false perceptions of real life. The adults in our students' lives, whether family or educators, can unknowingly facilitate the pressure of reaching certain expectations by comparing them with others. Every morning before I send my children off to school, I always remind them to try their best. If a C is their best that day on that assignment, that is ok. It does not mean that they should not aim for higher. They should give it all they got, and I would be proud of them. As an educator, I always tell my students the same thing. "Give me your best and only your very best." The high expectations trap is also perpetuated by a culture that values achievement and success above all else. This can create a sense of pressure to perform at a high level, even at the expense of mental and emotional well-being.

Conversely, the "high expectations trap" also refers to the phenomenon where educators and other authority figures hold marginalized students to lower expectations. These lower expectations can lead to a self-fulfilling prophecy where our students do not achieve their full potential due to a lack of belief in their abilities. A study by Mallette and Ruiz (2017) found that teachers' low expectations for African American and Latino students correlated with adverse academic outcomes, including lower achievement and higher rates of grade retention.

Setting realistic goals and prioritizing self-care is essential to avoid the high expectations trap. This may involve setting smaller, more attainable goals and celebrating each achievement along the way. It also involves recognizing the value of self-compassion and the importance of taking breaks and engaging in activities that promote mental and emotional well-being. It is vital for educators, families, and other authority figures to have high expectations for all students and to provide the necessary support to help them reach those expectations. This support can include providing resources and opportunities for academic and personal growth and actively challenging negative stereotypes and biases that may lead to low expectations (Dweck, 2006).

Do I Have High Expectations for My Students?

Educators with high expectations believe that all students can succeed, and they work to create a positive and inclusive learning environment that fosters academic achievement and personal growth (Ginsburg, 2017). Having high expectations for students means setting challenging but attainable goals and providing support and resources to help them reach those goals (Ginsburg, 2017). It involves recognizing and building on our students' strengths while identifying areas for growth and providing opportunities for improvement.

Research has consistently shown that having high expectations for students is associated with positive academic and behavioral outcomes. A meta-analysis of over 800 studies found that high teacher expectations positively affect student achievement, motivation, and self-esteem (Jussim & Harber, 2005). Similarly, a longitudinal study of middle school students found that students who had teachers with high expectations had greater academic gains in both math and reading compared to students with lower expectations (Borman & Dowling, 2010).

Having high expectations for students also involves providing opportunities for them to develop their skills and talents, as well as providing support and resources to overcome obstacles and challenges. This includes creating a supportive and inclusive classroom environment, providing effective feedback, and encouraging student engagement and participation (Ginsburg, 2017).

High expectations for our students are an essential component of effective instruction and can significantly impact student success and well-being. High expectations for all students, including marginalized students, is setting ambitious academic achievement goals and believing they can reach those goals. This includes providing the same challenging curriculum, high-quality instruction, and supportive learning environment as their more privileged peers. High expectations also involve recognizing and valuing each student's unique strengths and experiences and creating opportunities for them to succeed based on their interests and abilities (Gay, 2002). By having high expectations for all students, educators can help to promote equity and reduce the achievement gap between students from different backgrounds.

Do My Students Have High Expectations for Themselves?

Research suggests that marginalized students may internalize low expectations for themselves due to various factors, including negative stereotypes and limited exposure to high-achieving peers and role models (Steele, 2010). However, educators can help facilitate high expectations by using culturally responsive and strength-based approaches that recognize and build on each student's strengths and potential.

One crucial strategy for facilitating high expectations is to provide students with opportunities to set goals and track their progress over time (Zimmerman, 2008). This approach involves helping our students identify their strengths and areas for improvement and then working with them to develop a plan for achieving their goals. By empowering our students to take ownership of their learning, educators can help build their self-efficacy and motivation. As a classroom teacher, empowering our students to take ownership of their learning was a big deal for me, and it took a lot of work, but the return on my investment was worth it.

Another essential strategy is to provide our students with access to high-quality educational resources and opportunities, such as advanced coursework, extracurricular activities, and mentorship programs (National Equity Project, 2018). By exposing students to challenging and enriching experiences, educators can broaden their horizons and expand their sense of what is possible. Mentorship programs are crucial for marginalized students because they provide access to individuals who usually look like them and focus on building our students' positive perceptions of themselves.

Additionally, educators can use culturally responsive and strength-based approaches that recognize and value marginalized students' cultural backgrounds and experiences (Gay, 2010). This approach involves creating an inclusive and respectful classroom environment of diverse perspectives and provides opportunities for our students to connect their learning to their own lives and communities. Too often, the narrative for our students is to assimilate into the primary culture and what others believe they should be instead of getting to know themselves and being aware of their own culture.

Many marginalized students start by holding themselves to high expectations despite facing significant barriers to academic success (Covington, 2000; Steele, 1997). Some of our students have even higher expectations for themselves than their more privileged peers. However, these high expectations can be undermined by a lack of opportunities and resources and by negative stereotypes and biases that can influence how others perceive their abilities and potential (Simpkins et al., 2013). Therefore, educators and policymakers need to recognize and support the high expectations that marginalized students hold for themselves and provide them with the resources and opportunities they need to achieve their goals. Facilitating high expectations for marginalized students requires a multifaceted approach grounded in a deep understanding of each student's individual strengths and needs.

High Expectations for All Students

Research suggests that high expectations can be significant for marginalized students, who may face additional barriers to academic achievement (Ladson-Billings, 2006). However, it is essential to note that these expectations must be realistic and tailored to each student's needs and strengths. Educators must put in the work required to learn about who students are beyond the data if they hope to set realistic expectations with attainable goals.

One approach to setting high expectations for marginalized students is to adopt culturally responsive teaching (CRT) practices. A CRT approach emphasizes the importance of building strong relationships with students, recognizing and valuing their cultural identities and experiences, and using instructional strategies that are relevant and engaging (Gay, 2010). This approach involves creating an inclusive and respectful classroom environment of diverse backgrounds and experiences. It provides opportunities for our students to connect their learning to their own lives and communities. Yes, a culturally responsive education is part of the answer to helping our students overcome many of the barriers they face.

Another critical factor in setting high expectations for marginalized students is providing them with high-quality educational resources and opportunities (National Equity Project, 2018). This approach includes ensuring students have access to well-trained and culturally responsive educators, rigorous and relevant curricula, and high-quality instructional materials and technology. Our students are often served with outdated practices, curricula, and instructional materials. It is essential to understand that the resources and strategies must be current.

In addition, it is vital to recognize and address the systemic barriers that can contribute to achievement gaps for our students, such as inadequate funding for schools serving low-income communities, biased testing and assessment practices, and inadequate teacher preparation and professional development (Ladson-Billings, 2006). Systematic barriers are often harder to address but not impossible. Sometimes it takes just one person to open the door and shine the light on the issues. By addressing these broader issues, educators can help create a more equitable and inclusive education system that supports the success of all students.

Are My High Expectations for My Students Realistic?

To set realistic high expectations for students, educators should use various assessment methods to evaluate each student's current knowledge and skills and then work with the student to set challenging but attainable goals (Harrison, 2019). A relationship must also be developed to gain an understanding beyond the numbers found in the data. This approach involves creating a positive and inclusive learning environment that fosters academic achievement and personal growth while recognizing and building on students' strengths. Whatever the expectations are set, it should not be a standard for complacency. Just because our students hit the expectations we set for them, it does not mean we should not try to push them further.

One critical step in setting realistic high expectations is to establish clear learning goals and objectives for each lesson or unit and to communicate these goals to students in a meaningful and understandable way (Marzano & Kendall, 2007). Meaningful and clear communication involves breaking down complex concepts or skills into smaller, manageable steps that can be achieved over time. This approach can provide short-term motivation with a focused long-term vision.

Educators should also provide ongoing feedback and support to help students achieve their goals, including opportunities for practice and application and individualized instruction and assistance as needed (Black & Wiliam, 1998). This approach involves using formative assessment methods to monitor our students' progress and adjust instructional strategies. Feedback should not be a guessing game and should be as descriptive as possible and tailored.

In addition, educators should provide students with opportunities to reflect on their learning and set their own goals, which can help build their self-efficacy and motivation (Zimmerman, 2008). This approach involves encouraging our students to identify areas of strength and weakness, set goals for improvement, and monitor their progress over time. Promoting a growth mindset in students through reflection can help create the lifelong learner we all want our students to be. Setting realistic high expectations for students requires a tailored and individualized approach grounded in ongoing assessment and support and emphasizes the development of both academic and personal skills.

When we expect greatness from our students, we instill in them the confidence to believe in themselves and the courage to pursue their passions.

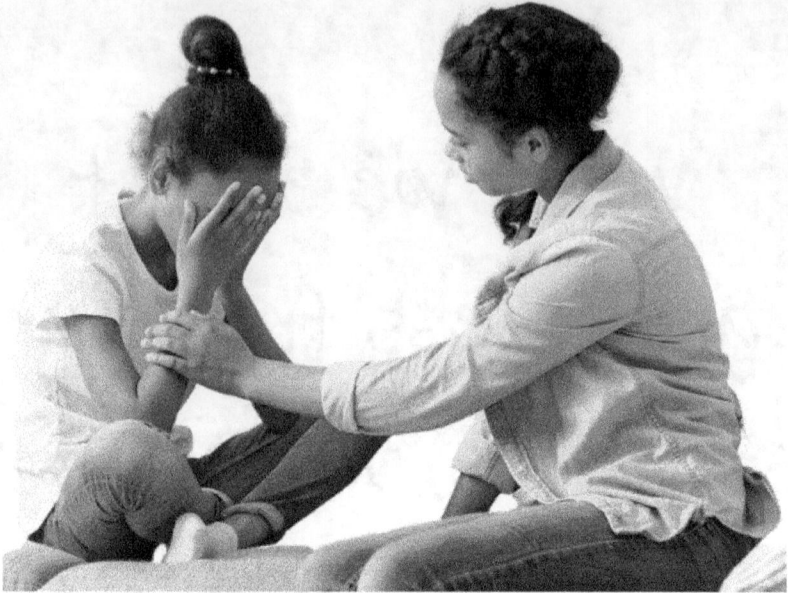

Chapter 6: Empathy and Positive Relationships

There lived a teen girl named Emy from a small and diverse town who lived in one of the poorer sections of town. She was a teen mom struggling to raise her beautiful 2-year-old daughter, Lilybeth, all alone. She was an English Language Learner who came to the USA only four years before. As if life hadn't thrown enough challenges at her, Emy's mother, Cindy, was dying of cancer. Emy was only eighteen, but the world's weight was already on her shoulders.

Despite the adversities, Emy tried her best to keep up with school. However, as her responsibilities mounted, her academic achievements started to suffer. She was often tired, struggling to balance her duties as a mother, a caretaker for her ailing mother, and a high school student. She often arrived at school with dark circles under her eyes, her hair disheveled, and her homework incomplete.

Emy's teachers and peers didn't understand her struggles, and they often judged her harshly. Emy built walls around herself, shutting everyone out. Her isolation grew deeper as her mother's health worsened. Despite the overwhelming odds, Emy refused to give up on her education. She knew graduating high school would provide a better future for her and Lilybeth.

As Emy's senior year ended, she realized she didn't have enough credits to graduate on time. She felt defeated and alone, but she wasn't willing to quit just yet. Emy decided to go back as a 5th-year senior, determined to earn her diploma to be a role model to her daughter and to make her mom proud.

At the beginning of Emy's fifth year, a new assistant principal, Mr. Rivera, joined the school. He was an empathetic man who genuinely cared for the well-being of each student. Mr. Rivera noticed Emy's struggles and saw through the walls she had built to protect herself. He also so the potential and resilience within her and made it his mission to help her succeed.

One day, Mr. Rivera called Emy into his office after she had a meltdown in one of her classes. He sat her down, told her he understood her difficulties and wanted to know how he could help her if she were willing. He told her, "I know that you have had difficulties in the past, but if you are ready to give it all you got, I will do everything in my power to make sure you have what you need to graduate." Overwhelmed by the kindness and understanding, Emy broke down in tears. It was the first time someone had truly seen through her behavioral issues and acknowledged her pain.

With Mr. Rivera's support, Emy started believing she could graduate. He arranged for her to receive tutoring and connected her with different support systems the city had available, including childcare for her daughter. Mr. Rivera even helped Emy find resources to help her mother get the proper care so that she could focus on her studies.

As the months passed, Emy's grades improved, and she began to feel like she would make it. She discovered newfound confidence, and everyone else started to notice. The walls she had built began to crumble, and Emy realized she was no longer alone. Teachers in the building saw her change and asked what more they could do to help.

On graduation day, Emy walked across the stage waving to Lilybeth, sitting on the sidelines, as she received her hard-earned diploma. As she posed for her picture on the stage, Emy glanced at Mr. Rivera with gratitude. She told him, "You will never truly know what you did for me. I will forever be thankful to you." He had shown her the kindness and empathy she desperately needed, helping her persevere through the darkest moments of her life. A few months after graduation, Emy returned to share with Mr. Rivera that she was starting a program to become a medical assistant, and she had a job as a receptionist at a doctor's office. Her mom was still fighting cancer but was in better spirits knowing that Emy would be ok.

Emy's story serves as a reminder that a little bit of empathy can go a long way. It can break down walls and help people overcome the most challenging obstacles. Because of Mr. Rivera's compassion and understanding, Emy was able to graduate high school and start a new chapter in her life, filled with hope and determination for a brighter future.

Empathy and Sympathy: There's a Difference.

Empathy and sympathy are often used interchangeably, but they are distinct concepts with different implications for social interactions. Empathy involves feeling what another person is feeling, while sympathy involves feeling sorry for another person's situation. Most times, people are not looking for sympathy; they are just hoping for a little bit of empathy. The same is true for our students. This book was not written to get people to feel bad for our students. On the contrary, this book was written to help people understand what our students are going through. Students who receive the support they need to overcome adversities are better because of it.

According to a study by Eisenberg and Miller (1987), empathy "involves sharing another person's emotions and taking an active interest in understanding his or her perspective" (p. 315). In contrast, sympathy "involves feeling concerned or sorrow for another's welfare" (p. 315). Empathy requires putting ourself in another person's shoes to understand their emotions and to support them through this difficulty. In contrast, sympathy acknowledges another person's emotions without necessarily understanding their feelings, and often the sympathizer goes into "fix-it" mode. Most of the time, people reach out because they want the support of a friend; they usually don't want the "fix-it" friend. They want a friend to say, "That sucks." There is a role for sympathy and empathy, but most people settle for sympathy because it is easier.

Knowing the difference between empathy and sympathy is important because it can affect how we interact with others. Empathy can help build stronger relationships and improve communication by demonstrating understanding and validating another person's feelings. On the other hand, sympathy can be perceived as condescending or dismissive if it is not accompanied by genuine concern and effort to understand the other person's perspective.

Our students are not looking for someone to feel sorry for them; they are looking for someone who cares enough to understand them and validate that their struggles are important too. They want someone to support them through their struggles. It is through our struggles that we grow the most. Often as adults, we dismiss teens' struggles. When we acknowledge them, we sometimes compare them to our own struggles and minimalize their impact. Understanding the difference can help us communicate effectively and build stronger relationships. Positive relationships with our students make a big difference and can often be all that is needed for them to succeed. As an educator, I would leverage my relationships with students to help them reach the academic achievement they are capable of.

Empathetic Students

Empathy in education refers to the ability of students to understand and respond to the emotions and perspectives of others. Empathy is a critical component of social and emotional learning (SEL). It is increasingly recognized as an essential skill for success today.

Empathy in education involves creating a safe and supportive learning environment where students can develop emotional intelligence and empathize with others. Developing emotional intelligence and empathy can be done through various activities, such as storytelling, role-playing, and group discussions, which helps our students to understand and appreciate different perspectives.

However, teaching empathy in education can be challenging. One of the main challenges is that empathy is not an innate skill and requires practice and reinforcement. Additionally, cultural differences, personal biases, and past experiences can impact students' ability to empathize with others.

Another challenge is that the emphasis on academic achievement often takes precedence over social and emotional learning. As a result, educators may not have the necessary training or resources to teach empathy effectively. Some educators do not know how to be empathic themselves, and we all know modeling is an important aspect of learning.

Despite these challenges, empathy in education is crucial for several reasons. First, research has shown that students with higher levels of empathy perform better academically and have better mental health outcomes (Lopes et al., 2011).

Second, empathy is essential for building positive relationships, leading to improved collaboration, teamwork, and conflict-resolution skills.

Third, empathy can help students develop a sense of global citizenship, where they are aware of and appreciate the diverse perspectives and experiences of others (Gehlbach et al., 2016).

Empathy in education is essential for creating a safe and supportive learning environment, building positive relationships, and promoting academic and social-emotional development in our students. While there are challenges to teaching empathy, efforts should be made to prioritize and integrate it into educational curriculums.

Students Need Empathetic Educators.

Students need empathetic educators because empathy is essential for building positive relationships, promoting student engagement and motivation, and improving academic outcomes. Educators who demonstrate empathy create a safe and supportive learning environment where our students feel understood, respected, and valued. Students often put-up brick walls, as seen in Emy's story, to see who cares enough and is willing to break through that wall.

Research has shown that teaching empathy positively correlates with student motivation, engagement, and academic achievement (Pekrun et al., 2017; Roorda et al., 2011). Additionally, empathetic educators can help students develop social-emotional skills crucial for success in school and life (Durlak et al., 2011).

Furthermore, empathetic educators can support students dealing with personal or family issues and help create a positive school climate by modeling respectful and compassionate behavior (Jennings & Greenberg, 2009).

Students need empathetic educators because empathy promotes positive relationships, student engagement and motivation, and academic outcomes. Empathetic educators can also help support our students' social-emotional development and create a positive school climate. Being empathetic can be difficult because it requires examining one's bias and changing who we are to benefit others. Not everyone can naturally see how helping others can help them.

Building Empathy

Developing empathy for our students can be a challenging but important task for educators. Empathy can help educators better understand and respond to their students' emotions, experiences, and perspectives, ultimately leading to improved relationships and academic outcomes. Strategies for developing empathy:

1.   Active Listening: Educators can develop empathy by actively listening to their students and paying attention to their nonverbal cues. Active Listening involves reflecting on what students say and asking clarifying questions to better understand their thoughts and feelings.

2.   Perspective-Taking: Educators can try to see things from their students' perspectives by considering their backgrounds, experiences, and cultural norms. Perspective-Taking can help educators better understand and appreciate their students' viewpoints.

3.   Reflection and Self-Awareness: Educators can develop empathy by reflecting on their own experiences and biases and how these may impact their interactions with our students. Reflection and Self-Awareness help educators be more aware of their own feelings and reactions and better respond to their students' needs.

Challenges to Building Empathy

Building student empathy fosters a positive classroom environment and promotes social-emotional learning. However, there can be challenges in nurturing empathy, particularly for marginalized students.

Some of these challenges include:

1. Diverse backgrounds and experiences: Students come from various backgrounds and have unique experiences, which can create misunderstandings or misinterpretations of others' feelings and perspectives (Gay, 2010). These misunderstandings or misinterpretations may be particularly true for marginalized students, who might feel disconnected from their peers due to cultural, linguistic, or socioeconomic differences.

2. Limited exposure to diversity: Students with limited exposure to diverse perspectives and experiences may find it challenging to understand and empathize with others (Allport, 1954). This challenge can be especially problematic for marginalized students, who may feel misunderstood or isolated in predominantly homogenous educational settings.

3. Emotional regulation and self-awareness: Developing empathy requires self-awareness and the ability to regulate one's emotions. Some students might struggle with emotional regulation or have limited self-awareness, hindering their ability to empathize with others (Brackett et al., 2011).

To overcome these challenges, educators can employ various strategies:

1. Culturally responsive instruction: By incorporating diverse perspectives, materials, and instructional strategies, educators can help students understand and appreciate different cultures and experiences, fostering empathy and reducing biases (Gay, 2010).

2. Promote perspective-taking: Encourage students to put themselves in others' shoes and consider diverse viewpoints through role-playing, discussions, or reflective writing assignments (Zimmerman, 2019). Perspective-taking can help students develop empathy for their peers, including marginalized students.

3. Social-emotional learning (SEL) programs: Implementing SEL programs in the classroom can help students develop self-awareness, emotional regulation, and empathy (Durlak et al., 2011). These programs typically involve explicit instruction, modeling, and practice of social-emotional skills.

4. Encourage open dialogue: Create a safe space for students to share their experiences and emotions, fostering understanding and empathy among peers (Melnick & Martinez, 2018). Open dialogue is particularly important for marginalized students, who might feel unheard or unsupported in the classroom.

5. Collaborative learning experiences: Engaging students in collaborative learning activities can help break down barriers and promote understanding among diverse groups of students (Gillies & Boyle, 2010). Collaboration can encourage empathy and support marginalized students in connecting with their peers.

By addressing these challenges and implementing targeted strategies, educators can foster empathy among our students, including those from marginalized backgrounds. Building empathy in the classroom contributes to a more inclusive, supportive, and understanding learning environment for all students.

Impact of Positive Student-Teacher Relationships

In this book, you may have noticed that there has not been much discussion on discipline or alternatives to discipline. Its absence is not because it is not an issue but due to the belief that discipline is a surface problem. Diving under the surface, we will find the underlining issues that discipline often covers up. A positive student-teacher relationship can help prevent the brick walls our students put up, bring to the surface the underlining problems, and allow us to get straight to the academic and behavioral issues. Positive teacher-student relationships significantly impact the classroom environment, student academic success, and school climate and culture.

Classroom Environment:

Positive relationships are pivotal in shaping the school and classroom environment, contributing to a supportive, inclusive, and engaging atmosphere that fosters learning (Roorda et al., 2011). These relationships can impact various aspects of the learning experience, such as student engagement, motivation, self-efficacy, and academic success (Hamre & Pianta, 2001).

A positive classroom environment can be characterized by mutual respect, open communication, and trust between educators and students (Cornelius-

White, 2007). Educators who form strong connections with their students can create an atmosphere where learners feel safe and valued, leading to increased participation and collaboration. These connections can result in a more positive and inclusive learning environment, promoting all students' academic success and well-being (Roorda et al., 2011).

In contrast, negative relationships can harm the school and classroom environment. A lack of connection and trust can lead to decreased student engagement, motivation, and academic performance (Hughes et al., 2008). Additionally, negative relationships can contribute to higher levels of conflict, disruptive behavior, and disorganization (Baker et al., 2008).

Marginalized students, such as those from minority backgrounds, low-income families, or with special needs, are particularly vulnerable to the effects of both positive and negative relationships. Positive relationships can provide crucial support and resources, promoting these students' academic success and social-emotional well-being (Croninger & Lee, 2001). Conversely, negative relationships may exacerbate the unique challenges marginalized students face, leading to further disparities in academic achievement (Suldo et al., 2016).

To counteract these adverse effects on academic achievement, educators should strive to develop culturally responsive instructional practices, which involve acknowledging and embracing the diverse backgrounds of their students (Gay, 2010). Culturally responsive instructional practices include incorporating culturally relevant materials, addressing social justice issues in the classroom, and fostering strong relationships with all students, particularly those from marginalized backgrounds.

Positive student-teacher relationships are vital in shaping an inclusive and supportive classroom environment that fosters academic success for all students. By contrast, negative relationships can hinder learning and exacerbate disparities for marginalized students. Thus, educators must develop strong connections with their students, utilizing culturally responsive instructional practices to ensure an inclusive and positive classroom environment.

Student Academic Success:

Positive relationships are crucial in promoting student academic success. These relationships can impact various aspects of learning, such as engagement, motivation, self-efficacy, and achievement (Roorda et al., 2011).

One of the primary ways positive relationships contribute to academic success is by fostering a sense of belonging and connection in the classroom (Hamre & Pianta, 2001). When students feel valued and supported by their educators, they are more likely to engage in learning activities, take risks, and persist in challenging tasks. This engagement can lead to improved academic outcomes (Fredricks et al., 2004).

Additionally, positive relationships can enhance students' motivation by nurturing their intrinsic interest in learning (Deci & Ryan, 2000). Educators who are responsive and attuned to their students' needs can tailor instruction to meet individual interests, promoting a sense of autonomy and competence. Their new sense of autonomy and competence can result in increased motivation, a key predictor of academic success (Wentzel, 1999).

Moreover, positive relationships can bolster students' self-efficacy or the belief in their ability to succeed in academic tasks (Bandura, 1993). When educators provide encouragement, constructive feedback, and support, students are more likely to develop a strong sense of self-efficacy, which has been linked to better academic performance (Zimmerman, 2000).

Marginalized students can particularly benefit from positive relationships. These students often face unique challenges in the educational setting, leading to disparities in academic achievement (Suldo et al., 2016). Strong relationships can mitigate these challenges by providing marginalized students with the support and resources they need to succeed academically (Croninger & Lee, 2001).

For instance, culturally responsive instructional practices can strengthen relationships and improve academic outcomes for marginalized students (Gay, 2010). By incorporating culturally relevant materials and addressing social justice issues in the school and classroom, educators can create an inclusive learning environment that fosters success for all students.

Positive relationships are vital in promoting academic success for all students, including marginalized populations. By fostering a sense of belonging, enhancing motivation, and supporting self-efficacy, educators can help our students overcome obstacles and achieve their full potential.

School Climate and Culture:

Positive relationships contribute significantly to a school's climate and culture, which can have far-reaching effects on students' academic success, social-emotional development, and overall well-being (Thapa et al., 2013). These relationships can foster a sense of belonging, mutual respect, and trust among students and staff, creating a supportive and inclusive environment (Roorda et al., 2011).

In contrast, negative relationships can lead to a hostile and disengaged school climate characterized by low levels of trust, high levels of conflict, and poor communication among students and staff (Baker et al., 2008). A hostile and disengaged school climate can result in decreased student engagement, higher rates of behavioral problems, and ultimately lower academic achievement (Hughes et al., 2008).

An empathetic school climate and culture, where teachers and staff prioritize understanding and responding to student's unique needs and experiences, can provide a nurturing and supportive environment that promotes students' overall well-being (Zins et al., 2007). This includes fostering social-emotional learning, enhancing resilience, and encouraging prosocial behaviors, which can help students navigate academic and personal challenges more effectively (Durlak et al., 2011).

Marginalized students can significantly benefit from an empathetic school climate and culture. By fostering positive relationships and promoting a culture of empathy, schools can create an inclusive environment supporting all students' success, particularly those from marginalized backgrounds (Gay, 2010). This supportive environment can help mitigate these students' unique challenges and contribute to more equitable educational outcomes (Suldo et al., 2016).

Positive relationships are essential in shaping a school's climate and culture. These relationships contribute to a supportive and empathetic environment that benefits all students, especially those from marginalized backgrounds. Conversely, negative relationships can adversely affect the school's climate and culture, leading to poor academic and social outcomes. By prioritizing empathy and fostering strong relationships with our students, schools can create a nurturing and inclusive environment that promotes success for all students.

Leveraging Positive Student-Teacher Relationships

Leveraging positive relationships in the school and classroom environment can lead to improved academic success and positively impact the school's climate and culture (Roorda et al., 2011). Educators can foster strong connections with our students that promote learning, engagement, and well-being by employing specific strategies.

1. Building rapport and trust: Educators can initiate positive relationships with students by demonstrating genuine care, empathy, and respect, which can contribute to a supportive classroom environment and enhance the school's climate and culture (Cornelius-White, 2007).

2. High expectations and feedback: High expectations for academic performance and behavior, coupled with constructive feedback, can promote academic success and encourage students to put forth their best efforts (Hattie & Timperley, 2007).

3. Encouraging collaboration and participation: Fostering a collaborative learning environment and promoting active participation can enhance students' engagement, leading to better academic outcomes and a more inclusive school climate (Gillies & Boyle, 2010).

4. Culturally responsive teaching: Implementing culturally responsive teaching practices can create a more inclusive classroom and positively impact the school's climate and culture by recognizing and valuing students' diverse backgrounds (Gay, 2010).

5. Individualized support: Providing targeted support to address individual student's needs can improve academic success and contribute to a supportive school culture that prioritizes the well-being of all students (Tomlinson, 2014).

By building positive relationships, educators can create a school and classroom environment that promotes academic success while positively influencing the school's climate and culture. These efforts can contribute to a more supportive, inclusive, and engaging educational setting that benefits all students, particularly those from marginalized backgrounds (Suldo et al., 2016).

Do I listen actively and without judgment when students express themselves, offering validation and support in response?

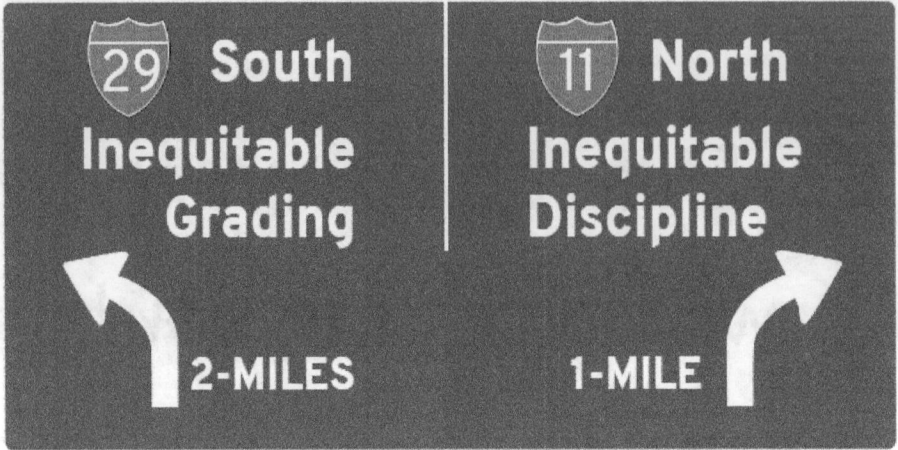

Chapter 7: A Tale of Two Old Systems of Inequity

The Grading System

The history of grading in education can be traced back to the 18th and 19th centuries when industrialization and urbanization led to the need for standardized education systems (Feldman, 2019). Before this time, education was primarily the purview of religious institutions, and assessment was often based on subjective judgments of individual teachers or clergy members.

In the late 19th century, as public schools became more common and compulsory education laws were implemented, the need for standardized assessments became more pressing. The development of norm-referenced tests, such as the Stanford-Binet Intelligence Scale and the Iowa Test of Basic Skills, provided a way to compare students' performance to a normative sample and identify those not meeting expected benchmarks (Feldman, 2019).

At the same time, grading systems began to develop as a way to provide feedback to students and parents on their progress and achievement. These grading systems were initially based on a binary pass/fail model. Still, they soon evolved to include letter grades, which provided more nuance and differentiation in assessing students' performance (O'Connor, 2019).

In the 20th century, the use of grades became more widespread. They began to be used not only as a measure of academic achievement but also as a means of controlling and motivating students' behavior (Feldman, 2019). This use of grades for control and punishment has been criticized for its adverse impacts on student motivation and engagement, as will be discussed later in the chapter.

In recent decades, there has been a growing movement towards alternative grading systems, such as standards-based grading, mastery-based grading, and competency-based grading. These alternative grading systems are designed to promote more equitable and accurate assessments of student learning and to reduce the impact of systemic biases in the grading system. The grading systems focus on students' mastery of specific learning objectives or competencies rather than accumulating points or completing assignments (Feldman, 2019).

What is Grading Equity? Why Does It matter?

Grading Equity is an approach that aims to create fair and unbiased grading practices in educational settings. This approach seeks to eliminate systemic barriers and biases that may unfairly impact student achievement, particularly for those from marginalized or historically underserved groups. Grading Equity emphasizes the importance of clear learning objectives, transparent evaluation criteria, and the use of multiple measures to assess student learning (Feldman, 2019).

Grading Equity matters for several reasons:

1. Promotes fairness and inclusivity: Grading Equity aims to reduce biases and disparities in grading that may arise from factors unrelated to students' academic abilities, such as race, gender, socioeconomic background, or language proficiency (Darling-Hammond et al., 2020). Educators can create a more inclusive learning environment by ensuring that all students are assessed equitably.

2. Enhances student motivation and engagement: When students perceive the grading system as fair, they are more likely to be motivated and engaged in their learning (Hulleman et al., 2010). Grading Equity can help foster a growth mindset, encouraging students to focus on learning and improvement rather than solely on their performance.

3. Improves learning outcomes: Research suggests that when grading practices are transparent and closely aligned with learning objectives, students are more likely to achieve higher levels of understanding (Wormeli, 2006). Grading Equity supports using formative assessments, which provide feedback to students on their learning progress, enabling them to address gaps in understanding and improve their performance.

4. Fosters social justice: Grading Equity can help address the systemic inequalities that persist in education by ensuring that all students, regardless of their background, have equal opportunities for success (Darling-Hammond et al., 2020). By removing barriers to achievement, educators can contribute to a more equitable society.

Grading Equity is a vital approach to assessment that promotes fairness, inclusivity, and improved learning outcomes. To address these systematic issues, grading equity emphasizes the importance of creating grading policies and practices sensitive to students' differences and designed to promote equitable outcomes. By adopting grading practices that account for students' diverse experiences and backgrounds, educators can ensure that all learners are given an equal opportunity to succeed, regardless of their race, ethnicity, socioeconomic status, or other factors. Educators can contribute to a more just and inclusive education system by implementing equitable grading practices.

Zeros Tell Us Nothing

Giving our students a zero has been found to be unfair and ineffective for several reasons. These reasons include the fact that zeros are mathematically disproportionate to other grades, that they do not accurately reflect student learning or progress, and that they can disproportionately impact marginalized students.

One key issue with giving students a zero is that zeros are mathematically disproportionate to other grades. Research has shown that using zeros can result in inflated grades and inaccurate evaluations of student learning. A single zero can significantly impact a student's overall grade (O'Connor, 2019). In addition, using zeros can create a sense of hopelessness and defeat among students, as they may feel that there is no way to recover from a single poor performance (Cohen, 2018).

Another issue with giving our students a zero is that they do not accurately reflect student learning or progress. Zeros do not provide meaningful feedback to students about what they need to improve on, and they do not account for the progress they have made over time (Cohen, 2018). Instead, zeros penalize students for not meeting a specific benchmark or deadline without considering the unique challenges and circumstances that students may be facing.

Finally, the use of zeros can disproportionately impact marginalized students. Research has shown that marginalized students are more likely to receive zeros than their more privileged peers due to systemic biases in the grading system and teacher evaluations (Feldman, 2019). This can result in further marginalization and disengagement among these students, who may already face a range of obstacles to academic success.

0-100 A Mathematical Flaw

The mathematical flaw of a 0-100 grading scale lies in the fact that it is not a true zero-based scale. This means that a grade of zero does not truly represent an absence of learning or performance but rather a failure to meet a specific benchmark or deadline. This mathematically flawed grading scale can lead to a distortion of our students' grades and an inaccurate representation of their overall performance (O'Connor, 2019).

Research has shown that using a 0-100 grading scale can result in inflated grades and inaccurate evaluations of student learning. A single zero can significantly impact a student's overall grade, even if they have performed well on other assignments or assessments (O'Connor, 2019). In addition, using a 0-100 grading scale can create a false sense of precision and objectivity when grades are often based on subjective judgments and biases (Feldman, 2019).

Moreover, using a 0-100 grading scale can also create an undue focus on the grade itself rather than on the learning and growth that the grade is meant to represent. This can lead to a "grade-centered" approach to education rather than a "learning-centered" approach, where students are more concerned with their grades than with their actual understanding of the material (Brookhart, 2018).

To address this flaw, some educators have proposed implementing a minimum grade policy, which would require teachers to assign a minimum grade to our students with minimal proficiency. The exact implementation of a minimum grade policy can vary. Still, it typically involves setting a minimum grade that teachers must assign to students who have demonstrated a basic understanding of the material (Feldman, 2019).

The rationale behind a minimum grade policy is that it would help to address the mathematical flaw of a 0-100 grading scale by ensuring that grades more accurately reflect student learning and performance. In addition, a minimum grade policy could help reduce systemic biases in the grading system, which can disproportionately impact marginalized students, by providing a minimum level of academic support and recognition for all students (Feldman, 2019).

However, it is important to note that implementing a minimum grade policy alone is insufficient to address all of the flaws and inequities in the grading system. As Feldman (2019) note, a minimum grade policy should be part of a larger effort to create a more equitable and effective grading system. A more effective system should also include ongoing feedback, multiple opportunities for our students to demonstrate their learning, and a focus on growth and improvement rather than just grades.

A Grading Scale That Emphasizes Learning

A 4-point or 5-point grading scale is considered a more equitable grading system than a traditional 0-100 scale because it allows for greater differentiation between levels of mastery and is less susceptible to the mathematical flaws and biases of the traditional system. Additionally, it provides clearer and more consistent feedback to our students, helping them to understand their progress and areas of the improvement more effectively (Feldman, 2019). The 4-point or 5-point scale typically uses descriptive language to indicate the level of mastery or understanding a student has achieved in a particular area rather than assigning a numerical grade based on a percentage or points system. This scale can help reduce the focus on achieving a certain score and instead emphasize the importance of understanding and applying knowledge and skills.

To implement a 4-point or 5-point grading scale, educators can use a rubric that outlines clear criteria for each level of mastery. Implementing a 4-point or 5-point grading scale involves creating clear and specific descriptors for each level of achievement, such as "exceeds expectations," "meets expectations," "approaching expectations," "partially meets expectations," and "not meeting expectations." These descriptors should be aligned with specific learning objectives or standards and provide clear criteria for evaluating student performance. Each level would have specific descriptions and criteria that clearly define what the student needs to do to achieve that level of mastery (Feldman, 2019).

Another way to implement a 4-point or 5-point grading scale is to combine letter grades and numerical scores. For example, a student might receive a letter grade of A, B, C, D, or F but with a corresponding numerical score of 4, 3, 2, 1, or 0. This approach allows for more nuance and differentiation in grading while providing a clear and easily understandable system for students and families (Wormeli, 2006).

One potential benefit of a 4-point or 5-point grading scale is that it can reduce the potential for bias or subjectivity in grading. Because the descriptors are clearly defined and aligned with specific standards, our students and parents can better understand what is expected of them and what they need to do to achieve success. When our students understand what is expected, it can also help to reduce anxiety and stress for students who may feel overwhelmed by the pressure to achieve a certain numerical grade.

To effectively implement a 4-point or 5-point grading scale, educators may need to engage in professional development to become familiar with the new grading system and develop effective assessment practices. It may also be necessary to communicate clearly with students and families how the new grading system works and what it means for their learning and progress (Feldman, 2019). Educators should be trained to develop clear descriptors and criteria for each level of achievement. They should communicate these criteria to our students at the beginning of each assignment or grading period. Ongoing feedback and support based on these criteria can help students understand their progress and improve as needed.

Overall, a 4-point or 5-point grading scale can help to promote more equitable and accurate assessments of student learning. Still, it requires a significant shift in thinking and practice from traditional grading systems.

Grades Are Not a Classroom Management Tool

Grades are essential for measuring student learning because they summarize a student's mastery of the content and skills taught in a course. However, grades should not be used to control students' behaviors or as a tool for punishment or reward, as this can have negative consequences for student motivation, engagement, and learning.

Using grades to control and punish our students can perpetuate disparities and inequalities, particularly for marginalized students. Research has shown that these students are more likely to receive lower grades and be subject to disciplinary actions than their peers, which can impact their opportunities and outcomes (Losen & Gillespie, 2012; Skiba et al., 2011a).

Additionally, using grades as a tool for control and punishment can create a negative cycle where students may disengage from learning and become more likely to exhibit problematic behaviors, which can further impact their grades and opportunities (Skiba et al., 2011a). Using grades in this way can be particularly detrimental for marginalized students who may face additional stressors and challenges outside school.

Research has shown that extrinsic motivation, such as the desire to earn a good grade or avoid a bad grade, can undermine students' intrinsic motivation and lead to a focus on performance goals rather than learning goals (Deci et al., 2001). This form of motivation can result in a shallow approach to learning, where our students may prioritize memorization or test-taking strategies over a deeper understanding and application of concepts.

Furthermore, using grades as a tool for control or punishment can lead to feelings of anxiety, stress, and pressure among students, which can also undermine their motivation and engagement (Schneider & Preckel, 2017). These feelings can create a negative cycle where students may be less likely to engage in learning activities or take risks in their learning for fear of negative consequences, which can further impact their learning outcomes.

Instead, grades should be used to provide feedback to students on their learning progress, identify areas of strength and improvement, and guide instructional decisions. By focusing on the learning goals and using grades as a measure of progress towards those goals, educators can promote intrinsic motivation and foster a deeper approach to learning (Deci et al., 2001).

It is crucial to address the disparities by promoting equitable grading practices based on clear, objective criteria and providing opportunities for student feedback and self-reflection. Educators should also be trained to recognize and address implicit biases and stereotypes impacting grading and discipline decisions (Losen & Gillespie, 2012).

Using grades as a means to assess student learning holds significant value. However, it is crucial to prevent the misuse of grades for controlling or punishing our students, as this can adversely affect motivation, engagement, and the learning process. Building intrinsic motivation is the best way to address academic and behavioral challenges.

The Discipline System

When I set out to write this book, I initially struggled with whether to include school discipline. After all, the issue of discipline is a surface-level problem that can be positively impacted by addressing the underlying issues that our marginalized students face. However, I ultimately decided that it was important to address the topic of school discipline because it is an oppressive system that affects our students daily, particularly our marginalized students.

The high use of exclusionary discipline practices such as suspension and expulsion and significant disparities in discipline rates by race, gender, and other factors characterizes the school discipline system. These disparities are not solely a result of differences in student behavior but are also rooted in systemic issues related to bias, discrimination, and unequal treatment. Moreover, exclusionary discipline practices have been linked to adverse student outcomes, such as an increased likelihood of dropping out, lower academic achievement, and negative involvement in the criminal justice system.

It is essential to recognize that the school discipline system is just one of many systems of oppression that our students face. Addressing the underlying issues contributing to disciplinary issues, such as poverty and systemic racism, is necessary to create a fair and equitable school system. However, it is also important to address the immediate impacts of the school discipline system on students' lives.

By understanding the complex and interconnected issues surrounding school discipline, we can work towards creating a truly equitable and just system for all students. The rest of the chapter will explore the historical context and current state of school discipline. We will also look at the impact of exclusionary discipline practices, alternatives to exclusionary discipline, and the role of bias in school discipline.

Inequities in School Discipline

The school discipline system is a critical aspect of the education system that plays a crucial role in shaping students' experiences. However, the current disciplinary system is fraught with inequities disproportionately affecting marginalized students. As a result, it is critical to discuss the injustices of the school discipline system to understand their impact on our students and identify solutions to address these inequities.

Studies have consistently shown that students of color and students with disabilities are disproportionately affected by harsh disciplinary practices such as suspension and expulsion (Losen & Skiba, 2010; Skiba et al., 2011b). In particular, Black students are suspended at three times higher rates than White students (Losen & Skiba, 2010). These disparities are not simply a result of differences in student behavior but are rooted in systemic issues related to bias, discrimination, and unequal treatment (Skiba et al., 2011b).

Moreover, exclusionary discipline practices such as suspension and expulsion have been linked to adverse outcomes such as academic failure, increased likelihood of dropping out, and involvement in the criminal justice system (Krezmienet al., 2006; Rumberger, 2011). These adverse outcomes can have long-term implications for students, particularly those already marginalized.

It is essential to discuss the school discipline system's inequities and identify alternative disciplinary approaches that promote positive student behavior while addressing systemic inequities. In doing so, educators, policymakers, and other stakeholders can work towards creating a more just and equitable education system that provides all students with the opportunity to succeed.

Historical Context of School Discipline

The historical context of school discipline in the United States can be traced back to the 19th century when public schools were first established. During this period, schools focused on instilling discipline and obedience in students, and educators used physical punishment to maintain order (Kahan, 1996). However, attitudes towards discipline in schools began to shift over time, and a more punitive approach emerged.

In the 1960s and 1970s, schools began adopting zero-tolerance policies in response to concerns about rising school violence and drug use (Skiba & Knesting, 2001). Zero-tolerance policies mandated automatic and severe disciplinary consequences for any student who engaged in certain behaviors, such as possession of drugs or weapons, regardless of the severity of the offense (Skiba & Knesting, 2001). These policies were intended to send a strong message that such behaviors would not be tolerated in schools. However, they also significantly increased the use of exclusionary discipline practices such as suspension and expulsion (Skiba et al., 2011b).

The shift towards a punitive approach to school discipline has been criticized for disproportionately impacting marginalized students. Studies have shown that students of color, particularly Black students are more likely to be disciplined and severely disciplined than White students (Losen & Skiba, 2010; Skiba et al., 2011b). Moreover, research has suggested that implicit bias on the part of teachers and administrators may play a role in these disparities (Okonofua et al., 2016).

In recent years, there has been a growing recognition of the need to reform the school discipline system to address these inequities. The increasing need to improve the system has led to the development of alternative disciplinary approaches, such as restorative justice practices and positive behavior interventions and supports (PBIS) (Skiba et al., 2011b). These approaches aim to promote positive student behavior while addressing the root causes of disciplinary issues and reducing the use of exclusionary discipline practices.

Current State of School Discipline

The high use of exclusionary discipline practices such as suspension and expulsion and significant disparities in discipline rates by race, gender, and other factors characterizes the current state of school discipline in the United States. According to Office for Civil Rights data, in the 2015-2016 school year, more than 2.7 million students received at least one out-of-school suspension, and approximately 100,000 students were expelled (U.S. Department of Education, 2018).

Moreover, students of color and students with disabilities are disproportionately affected by harsh disciplinary practices. Not only has research shown that Black students are suspended at rates higher than White students, but it is also true that students with disabilities are also more likely to be disciplined than general education students (Losen & Skiba, 2010; Skiba et al., 2011b). While these factors are discussed for male students, additional research has shown that girls of color are more likely to be disciplined than White girls (Morris, 2016).

These disparities are not solely a result of differences in student behavior but are also rooted in systemic issues related to bias, discrimination, and unequal treatment (Skiba et al., 2011b). For example, a study by the Government Accountability Office found that Black students, particularly boys, were more likely to be disciplined for subjective offenses such as "disrespect" or "disruption," which are more susceptible to bias in disciplinary decision-making (GAO, 2018).

Furthermore, using exclusionary discipline practices has been linked to adverse student outcomes, such as an increased likelihood of dropping out, lower academic achievement, and involvement in the criminal justice system (Krezmien et al., 2006; Rumberger, 2011). These adverse outcomes can have long-term implications for students, particularly those already marginalized.

Recently, there has been a growing recognition of the need to reform the school discipline system to address these inequities. Some schools and districts have begun to reduce discipline without addressing the problems, affecting school climate and culture. However, some schools and districts have started implementing alternative disciplinary approaches such as restorative justice practices and positive behavior interventions and supports (PBIS) to reduce exclusionary discipline practices and promote positive student behavior (Skiba et al., 2011b).

Impact of Exclusionary Discipline

Exclusionary discipline practices such as suspension and expulsion have been linked to adverse outcomes for our students, particularly those already marginalized. These practices are associated with a range of adverse outcomes, including an increased likelihood of dropping out, lower academic achievement, and involvement in the criminal justice system (Krezmien et al., 2006; Rumberger, 2011).

One of the primary adverse outcomes associated with exclusionary discipline is academic disengagement. Research has shown that students suspended or expelled are more likely to experience academic difficulties, such as lower grades and test scores, and are more likely to drop out of school (Krezmien et al., 2006; Rumberger, 2011). This can have long-term implications for students' success in postsecondary education and the workforce.

Moreover, exclusionary discipline practices can also contribute to the school-to-prison pipeline, particularly for marginalized students. Studies have shown that students suspended or expelled are more likely to become involved in the criminal justice system and that these effects are more pronounced for students of color (Skiba et al., 2011b). For example, a study by the Civil Rights Project found that Black students who were suspended or expelled were three times more likely to have contact with the juvenile justice system in the following year (Losen & Skiba, 2010).

Exclusionary discipline practices can also negatively impact students' mental health and well-being. Research has shown that suspended or expelled students are more likely to experience depression, anxiety, and other mental health issues (American Psychological Association, 2018). Moreover, the stress and trauma associated with these disciplinary practices can also affect students' relationships with educators and peers, further contributing to disengagement and negative outcomes.

Alternatives to Exclusionary Discipline

In recent years, there has been a growing recognition of the need to move away from exclusionary discipline practices such as suspension and expulsion and towards alternative disciplinary approaches that promote positive student behavior while addressing the root causes of disciplinary issues. Some examples of alternative disciplinary strategies implemented in schools and districts include restorative justice practices and positive behavior interventions and supports (PBIS).

Restorative justice practices are based on the principles of accountability, repair, and relationship-building (Wachtel, 2013). In schools, restorative justice practices typically involve bringing together students engaged in a conflict or harm with a trained facilitator to discuss the incident, its impact, and ways to repair damage and restore relationships. These practices aim to shift the focus from punishment to repairing harm and promoting positive relationships and have been associated with reductions in disciplinary referrals and improvements in school climate (Gregory et al., 2016).

Positive behavior interventions and supports (PBIS) is a systemic approach to promoting positive student behavior. It involves identifying and teaching positive behaviors, reinforcing them through positive feedback and rewards, and providing additional support for students who need it (Sugai et al., 2010). PBIS effectively reduces the use of exclusionary discipline practices and improves school climate (Bradshaw et al., 2010).

Other alternative disciplinary approaches implemented in schools and districts include peer mediation, counseling and mental health services, and trauma-informed practices (Gregory et al., 2016). These approaches aim to address the underlying factors contributing to disciplinary issues, such as trauma, mental health concerns, and lack of social-emotional skills.

The Role of Bias in School Discipline

Research has shown that implicit bias on the part of teachers and administrators can play a significant role in the disparities observed in school discipline rates, particularly by race and ethnicity (Okonofua et al., 2016). Implicit bias refers to the unconscious attitudes and stereotypes that individuals hold about certain groups of people, which can influence their behavior and decision-making.

Studies have found that teachers and administrators are more likely to view the same behavior as more severe and deserving of discipline when exhibited by students of color compared to White students (Skiba et al., 2011b). This bias can contribute to higher discipline rates for students of color and more severe disciplinary consequences, such as suspension and expulsion.

Moreover, research has shown that teachers and administrators may be more likely to view certain behaviors as problematic or disruptive based on their cultural background and experiences, which can further contribute to disparities in discipline rates (Losen & Skiba, 2010). For example, a student accustomed to speaking loudly or expressing themselves with gestures may be viewed as disrespectful by an educator unfamiliar with their cultural background.

Addressing bias in school discipline requires both awareness and action. Educating teachers and administrators about implicit bias and its impact on disciplinary decision-making is an essential first step. Additionally, schools and districts can implement training programs and resources that promote cultural competence and encourage using restorative justice practices and other alternative disciplinary approaches that address the root causes of disciplinary issues.

Like ripples on the water, behavioral problems are but a sign of deeper currents, let it be a reminder to look deeper, to seek the hidden emotions and experiences that lie beneath.

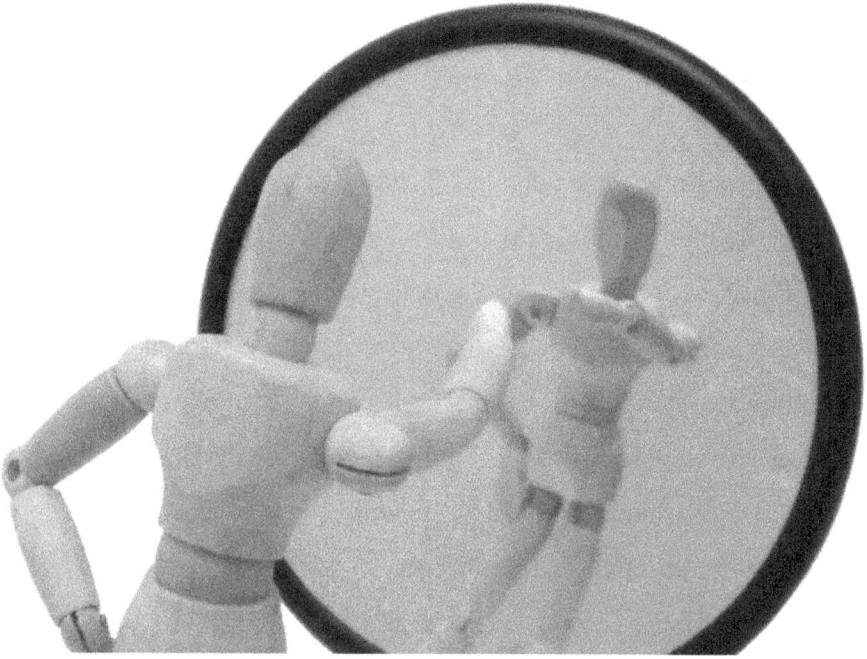

Chapter 8: Where Do We Go from Here?

Taking a Closer Look at Yourself.

Our greatest growth as individuals comes from taking a deep reflective look at our practices to see our personal truths. Reflection serves as a vital element in both personal and professional development for educators and other professionals, allowing them to evaluate their practices, values, biases, and beliefs; and to contemplate how these factors may affect their students, particularly those from marginalized backgrounds (Gay, 2010). Through reflection, educators can identify areas for improvement and adapt their instructional methods to create a more equitable learning environment to meet all students' needs.

Delving deeper into the challenges faced by marginalized students enables educators to gain insight into the unique experiences and obstacles our students might confront within the educational context. By committing to continuous reflective practice, educators can better comprehend the distinct difficulties these students face and modify their instructional approaches to ensure equal opportunities for success. Acknowledging the additional burdens placed upon marginalized students allows educators to empathize with their circumstances and cultivate a more supportive and inclusive learning atmosphere (Zimmerman, 2019).

By critically examining classroom practices, curricula, and assessment methods, educators can identify potential areas of bias and exclusion, and work towards creating a more culturally responsive and equitable educational experience for all students. Moreover, reflective practice empowers educators to challenge traditional instructional methods that may perpetuate systemic inequalities. Additionally, the reflective practice encourages collaboration among educators, fostering a community that values diversity and promotes social justice. The ongoing commitment to reflection and growth ultimately contributes to a more inclusive, equitable, and just education system.

Chapter 1 Reflection: Exploring My Students' Adversities

Educators can help alleviate barriers to success and promote academic growth by recognizing and addressing individual students' needs. Educators need to investigate potential hardships our students might encounter. Understanding these challenges enables them to provide targeted support, resources, and accommodations that foster a more inclusive and equitable learning environment. Furthermore, being aware of our students' difficulties can lead to the development of empathy and a deeper connection between educators and our students. This heightened understanding creates a more supportive and nurturing educational experience, allowing all students to thrive and reach their full potential.

The following questions should be considered to investigate potential hardships that our students might encounter and carry with them daily:

1. What are the socioeconomic backgrounds of the students I serve? Are any of them from low-income families or facing financial struggles?

2. Are any of our students experiencing homelessness or housing insecurity?

3. Do any students I serve have limited access to food, clothing, or other basic necessities?

4. Are any of our students dealing with mental health issues or other health concerns?

5. Do our students face discrimination or bullying based on race, gender, sexual orientation, religion, or other characteristics?

6. Have any of our students experienced trauma or adverse childhood experiences (ACEs)?

7. Are any of the students I serve dealing with family issues such as divorce, separation, or custody battles?

8. Do any of the students I serve have language barriers or limited English proficiency?

9. Are any of the students I serve dealing with challenges related to immigration status or refugee status?

10. Do our students have learning disabilities or special needs that require accommodations or support?

Exploring these questions can help us better understand the adversities the students we serve might face and guide us in working to create a supportive and inclusive classroom environment. It is in understanding that we can begin to address and support the adversities our students face.

Chapter 2 Reflection: Examining My Implicit Biases

Exploring and acknowledging our implicit biases is essential because they can unconsciously influence our thoughts, attitudes, and actions, often leading to unfair treatment or discrimination toward others. Recognizing these biases makes us more self-aware, promoting empathy, understanding, and a more inclusive environment. Furthermore, acknowledging implicit biases helps us to make more informed and objective decisions in various aspects of life, including education, the workplace, and interpersonal relationships. In doing so, we can work towards dismantling systemic inequalities and fostering a more equitable and just society for everyone.

To examine our implicit biases, here are a few questions we could explore:

1. What assumptions do I make about the students I serve based on their race, gender, religion, or other characteristics?
2. How might my own cultural background and experiences influence my interactions with our students from different cultures or backgrounds?
3. Do I have any prejudices or biases that might affect my interactions with certain students I serve?
4. How do I respond to students who challenge my assumptions or beliefs?
5. Do I treat all our students equally, or do I have any favorites or biases?
6. How do I respond to the students I serve who exhibit behavior outside of my cultural norms or expectations?
7. Do I give the students opportunities to share their own cultural perspectives and experiences in the classroom?
8. How do I respond to our students from disadvantaged backgrounds or who have experienced trauma?
9. Am I aware of any implicit biases that I might have, and how do I work to overcome them?
10. Do I make assumptions about the students I serve academic abilities based on their background or prior performance?

Investigating students' potential hardships is crucial, allowing educators to provide targeted support and promote an equitable learning environment. These understandings foster empathy and strengthen the teacher-student connection, enabling students to thrive and reach their full potential.

Chapter 3 Reflection: Assessing Injustices in the Learning Environment

Examining the disparities that exist in school and classroom communities is essential for educators, as it enables them to identify and address systemic inequalities that may hinder students' academic success and well-being. By scrutinizing these disparities, educators can develop targeted strategies and interventions to create a more inclusive, supportive, and equitable learning environment for all students, regardless of their background or circumstances. Furthermore, understanding these disparities can encourage collaboration among educators, administrators, and policymakers to develop comprehensive solutions that promote social justice and equal opportunities for every student. This proactive approach fosters a more diverse and vibrant educational community, enriching the learning experience for everyone involved.

These are self-inquiry questions that individuals can utilize to scrutinize the disparities that exist in the school and classroom:

1. Are all students given equitable opportunities to learn and succeed in my school and classroom?

2. Are our students from marginalized groups given the same opportunities and resources as their peers?

3. Do any of our school or classroom policies or practices disproportionately affect certain students or groups of students?

4. Are all students held to the same behavioral expectations, or are some students more likely to be disciplined than others?

5. Are students from marginalized groups represented in the curriculum and materials used in the classroom?

6. Do I use inclusive language and avoid stereotypes and biases in my instruction?

7. Do I make an effort to learn about and address the cultural differences and diverse experiences of my students?

8. Do I recognize and challenge power dynamics in the classroom, such as teacher-centered learning or student-teacher power imbalances?

9. Am I aware of and working to combat systemic racism, sexism, homophobia, ableism, or other forms of oppression within the school or education system?

10. Am I providing opportunities for students to advocate for themselves and others and to participate in social justice education and activism?

By exploring these questions, anyone can identify and work to address injustices within their schools and classrooms and create a more equitable and inclusive learning environment for all students.

Chapter 4 Reflection: The World Our Students Live In.

Educators must reflect on their understanding of students living in a world of instant gratification because this context can significantly influence students' learning behaviors, expectations, and engagement. By acknowledging the impact of the digital age on students' lives, educators can develop targeted strategies to motivate and support learners in a way that aligns with their experiences and needs. This may involve incorporating technology into instructional methods, fostering a growth mindset, and emphasizing the value of patience, persistence, and resilience in the learning process. Reflection also helps educators recognize the potential pitfalls of instant gratification, such as diminished attention spans or a reduced capacity for deep learning. It enables them to adapt their instructional practices accordingly. By guiding students through these challenges, educators can empower them to develop valuable skills and habits that will contribute to their long-term success in both academic and personal spheres.

Take a look at these questions that we can ask ourselves to reflect on our understanding of addressing the challenges of teaching students living in a world of instant gratification and to guide us in motivating our students:

1. Do I understand the impact of instant gratification on our students' motivation and learning?
2. Am I aware of how technology and social media shape our students' expectations and behaviors?

3. What strategies do I use to engage and motivate students who are used to getting what they want quickly and easily?

4. Do I use a variety of instructional strategies and technologies that cater to different learning styles and preferences?

5. How do I provide opportunities for our students to build self-discipline, perseverance, and self-gratification?

6. Am I setting clear expectations and providing regular feedback to help students monitor their progress and stay on track?

7. Do I provide our students with meaningful and relevant learning experiences that connect with their interests and passions?

8. Am I aware of our students' emotional and social needs and providing them with support and guidance when needed?

9. How do I communicate with parents and guardians about the challenges and opportunities that instant gratification presents in school and the classroom?

10. Do I model the behaviors and values I want our students to emulate, such as curiosity, persistence, and a growth mindset?

Reflecting on these questions can help educators better understand their students' perspectives and challenges and develop effective strategies to motivate and engage them in the learning process.

Chapter 5 Reflection: Expectations that Drive

It is crucial for educators to evaluate whether they hold high or low expectations for their students and if they instill a sense of high attainable expectations in their students themselves, as expectations play a significant role in shaping students' self-esteem, motivation, and academic achievement. High expectations from educators can inspire students to challenge themselves, persevere through difficulties, and believe in their ability to succeed. Conversely, low expectations can lead to a self-fulfilling prophecy, wherein students internalize these expectations and underperform, hindering their growth potential. By reflecting on and adjusting their expectations as needed, educators can foster a positive and supportive learning environment that encourages students to reach their full potential. Additionally, instilling highly attainable expectations empowers students to set ambitious yet realistic goals, leading to greater self-efficacy, resilience, and long-term success in their educational journey and beyond.

Consider the following questions for self-reflection to determine whether one holds high or low expectations for their students and whether they instill a sense of high attainable expectations in their students for themselves:

1. How do I define high expectations for our students, and what specific goals do I set for them?

2. Am I aware of my own biases and assumptions about our students' abilities and potential, and how do these influence my expectations?

3. Do I consistently communicate my high expectations to our students and provide them with clear feedback on how to meet these expectations?

4. Do I give our students opportunities to take risks, learn from failure, and build resilience to pursue their goals?

5. Do I differentiate instruction to meet each student's individual needs and interests while maintaining high standards for all?

6. Am I aware of and working to address systemic inequality and injustice that may affect our students' academic success?

7. Do I model high expectations for myself as an educator and continuously seek to improve my skills and knowledge to support our students better?

8. Do I involve our students in setting their own goals and developing strategies for achieving them, and do I celebrate their successes and progress along the way?

9. How do I respond to struggling students to meet high expectations, and do I provide them with the necessary support and resources to succeed?

10. Do I consistently hold myself accountable to high ethical and professional standards and seek feedback and support from colleagues, mentors, and other stakeholders to improve my practice?

By reflecting on these questions, educators can better understand their expectations for students and themselves as educators and work to promote a culture of high expectations, achievement, and growth in the classroom.

Chapter 6 Reflection: Relationships of Understanding

It is vital for educators to reflect on the differences between empathy and sympathy, as understanding these concepts plays a crucial role in fostering positive relationships with students. Empathy involves putting oneself in another's shoes and genuinely understanding their feelings and experiences. In contrast, sympathy is a more superficial acknowledgment of another's emotions or difficulties without truly comprehending their perspective. By embracing empathy in their interactions with students, educators can develop stronger connections and foster a sense of trust and understanding, leading to a more supportive and inclusive learning environment. Reflection on these concepts enables educators to recognize and address any shortcomings in their emotional connections with students, ultimately enhancing their ability to respond effectively to students' needs. Cultivating empathetic relationships also empowers students to be more open about their challenges and aspirations, allowing educators to provide targeted guidance and encouragement that promotes personal growth, academic achievement, and overall well-being.

Here are some questions that we can ask ourselves to reflect on our understanding of the differences between empathy and sympathy to guide us in building positive relationships with our students:

1. How do I define empathy and sympathy, and why is it important for me to know the difference?

2. How do I communicate with our struggling students, and do I tend to sympathize or empathize with them?

3. Am I aware of my own emotions and biases when interacting with students facing challenges?

4. Do I make an effort to understand and relate to our students' experiences and perspectives, and how do I demonstrate this in my instructional practices?

5. Do I provide opportunities for our students to share their thoughts and feelings in a safe and supportive environment?

6. How do I respond to students in emotional distress and validate their feelings without pitying or condescending to them?

7. Do I recognize and address systemic issues and structural inequalities that may contribute to our students' struggles?

8. Am I open to learning from and being challenged by our students, and do I value their unique talents, cultures, and identities?

9. How do I model empathy and positive relationships with our students, and do I hold myself accountable to high ethical and professional standards?

10. Do I continuously reflect on my teaching practices and seek feedback from my students, colleagues, and mentors to improve my empathy and relationship-building skills?

Educators can better understand the role of empathy and sympathy in building positive relationships with students and create a more compassionate and supportive learning environment by reflecting truthfully on the questions presented.

Chapter 7 Reflection: Systems of Oppression

Grade the Learning

Educators must evaluate whether their grading practices are fair and provide students with opportunities to demonstrate their mastery of standards in a way that meets them where they are, as equitable assessment is vital for promoting an inclusive and supportive learning environment. Fair grading practices ensure that all students, regardless of their background or circumstances, are assessed based on their understanding and abilities rather than factors unrelated to their academic achievement. By providing diverse opportunities for students to showcase their knowledge and skills, educators can accommodate different learning styles and experiences, enabling students to engage with the material in a way that best suits their needs. Evaluating and adjusting grading practices to promote fairness and equity contributes to a more inclusive educational experience, fostering students' motivation, engagement, and academic growth. Ultimately, fair and equitable grading practices empower students to reach their full potential and support the development of a diverse and thriving learning community.

Consider these reflective questions to evaluate whether grading practices are fair and provide students with opportunities to demonstrate their mastery of standards in a way that meets them where they are:

1. How do I define equitable grading practices, and what specific criteria do I use to evaluate student performance?

2. Am I aware of my own biases and assumptions that may affect how I evaluate student work, and how do I work to mitigate these biases?

3. Do I provide students with clear and consistent grading policies and expectations and communicate these policies to students and their families?

4. Do I provide students with multiple opportunities to demonstrate mastery of learning standards and allow them to revise and improve their work based on feedback?

5. Do I differentiate instruction and assessment to meet each student's individual needs and interests while maintaining rigorous academic standards?

6. Am I aware of and working to address systemic inequality and injustice that may affect our students' academic performance?

7. Do I use a variety of assessment methods, such as formative and summative assessments, performance tasks, projects, and portfolios, to evaluate student learning and growth?

8. Do I provide our students with timely and meaningful feedback on their work, and do I use this feedback to guide instruction and support student learning?

9. Am I transparent about my grading practices and policies, and do I involve our students in setting and tracking progress toward their goals?

10. How do I continuously reflect on and improve my grading practices to ensure they are equitable, supportive, and effective in promoting our students' success?

Through contemplation of these questions, an individual can gain deeper insight into their grading practices and strive to foster equitable assessment and grading approaches that acknowledge and accommodate all students' varied needs and abilities.

Digging Deeper than Exclusion

Reflection is a powerful tool for self-assessment and growth. In the context of school discipline, it is essential for all stakeholders, from teachers to policymakers, to engage in reflection to assess their current practices and policies and move toward a more equitable system that reduces the use of exclusionary discipline. These ten reflection questions are designed to prompt deep reflection on various aspects of the school discipline system, including bias, restorative justice practices, and stakeholder involvement. By engaging in regular reflection and assessment, stakeholders can create a more supportive and positive learning environment for all students.

1. Am I aware of the potential biases and stereotypes that may be influencing my disciplinary decisions?
2. How do I communicate with students and parents/guardians about discipline policies and procedures?
3. Do I utilize positive behavioral interventions and supports (PBIS) to create a positive and supportive school culture?
4. Am I consistently implementing restorative justice practices to address conflict and harm?

5. Do I involve all stakeholders, including students, families, and community members, in developing and implementing discipline policies and practices?

6. How am I monitoring and evaluating the effectiveness of my discipline policies and practices?

7. Am I collecting and analyzing discipline data by race, gender, disability status, and other factors to identify and address disparities?

8. How am I addressing the root causes of discipline issues, such as poverty and trauma, through counseling and other support services?

9. Am I seeking professional development opportunities on cultural competence, implicit bias, and restorative justice to improve my discipline practices?

10. How can I collaborate with community organizations, law enforcement, and other stakeholders to address discipline issues holistically?

Reflecting on the discipline practices and policies in schools is critical to creating a safe and supportive environment for all students. By engaging in regular reflection and assessment, all stakeholders can work towards creating a more equitable and just system that prioritizes the needs of students and reduces the use of exclusionary discipline practices. The reflection questions are designed to prompt deep self-assessment and growth in school discipline.

Getting Into the Arena

Theodore Roosevelt once said, "It is not the critic who counts; not the man who points out how the strong man stumbles, or where the doer of deeds could have done them better. The credit belongs to the man who is actually in the arena..." (Roosevelt, 1910). Brene Brown, a renowned researcher and author, has built upon this idea, emphasizing the importance of embracing vulnerability and daring to step into the arena of life (Brown, 2012).

We all face moments when we want to take action, make a change, or embark on a new journey, but we find ourselves held back by fear or uncertainty. How do we muster the courage to take that first step and enter the arena?

First, we must recognize that vulnerability is not a weakness but a strength. Embracing vulnerability means acknowledging our fears and insecurities and still choosing to step forward, knowing there is power in being seen and heard. As Brene Brown states, "Vulnerability is not winning or losing; it's having the courage to show up and be seen when we have no control over the outcome" (Brown, 2012).

Next, we must cultivate self-compassion. In times of uncertainty, we must be kind to ourselves and remember that we all stumble and experience setbacks. The same must be true for our students, and it is up to us to instill self-compassion through modeling and supporting them through their stumbles and setbacks. By practicing self-compassion, we create a safe space for ourselves to learn, grow, and build resilience (Neff, 2011). A safe space that becomes open so our students can learn, grow, and build resilience.

Finally, we must seek support from others. Surrounding ourselves with people who believe in us, encourage us, and challenge us can be instrumental in giving us the courage to step into the arena. We are not meant to face life's challenges alone; we are stronger together (Brown, 2012). Our students are young and impressionable. Believe in them, encourage them, and challenge them.

In order to show my support and provide you with the required resources to step into the arena, I have created next steps for stakeholder groups, enabling participation in the reform of our education system that is vital for all students.

Next Steps for Teachers

Embracing change and stepping into the realm of creating a more inclusive and equitable learning environment can be both challenging and rewarding. Remember that our willingness to adapt and grow will profoundly impact our students' lives, fostering their success and well-being. By being open to new ideas and perspectives, you become a catalyst for positive transformation, empowering our students to thrive in an ever-changing world. Teachers are the single most critical factor in a student's academic success. You are an important factor in this work; many of our students need you to jump into the arena. Here are suggested steps that teachers can take in their own classrooms to create a more inclusive and equitable learning environment using the Kotter 8-Step Process for Leading Change (Kotter, 1996) as a basis:

1. The first step in creating an inclusive and equitable learning environment is to become aware of the challenges and issues affecting students' learning and success. Teachers can engage in ongoing professional development, participate in diversity and inclusion training, and seek out resources and research on creating equitable learning environments. (Gorski, 2018).

2. The next step is to develop a desire and motivation to create a more inclusive and equitable learning environment. Teachers can reflect on their own biases and assumptions and work to develop empathy and understanding for their students' experiences and perspectives. (Bell & Lederman, 2020).

3. Teachers must have the knowledge and skills to create an inclusive and equitable learning environment. This may involve learning about cultural responsiveness, trauma-informed practices, and strategies for supporting students from diverse backgrounds. (Lindsey et al., 2013).

4. Teachers must develop the ability to implement inclusive and equitable classroom practices. These practices should involve creating a welcoming and supportive classroom environment,

providing differentiated instruction and assessment, and using culturally responsive teaching strategies. (Gay, 2018).

5. Finally, teachers must reinforce and sustain their efforts to create an inclusive and equitable learning environment. An inclusive and equitable learning environment should involve seeking out feedback from students and colleagues, evaluating the impact of their practices, and continuously reflecting on and improving their teaching strategies. (Lindsey et al., 2013).

Next Steps for Administrators

School administrators should be open to change and step into the arena of creating a more inclusive and equitable learning environment. It is essential in shaping the future of education. Your adaptability and vision will inspire teachers and staff to work collaboratively, positively impacting students' lives. Embrace new perspectives and ideas, and together, let's build a nurturing educational community that empowers every student to reach their full potential. Be a supportive instructional leader first and a disciplinarian last. Here are the steps that school administrators can take to create a more inclusive and equitable learning environment.

1. Establish a sense of urgency: The first step in creating a more inclusive and equitable learning environment is to establish a sense of urgency among school stakeholders about the need for change. Administrators can communicate the importance of diversity, equity, and inclusion in education and the potential impact of not addressing these issues. (Senge, 1990).

2. Form a powerful coalition: Administrators should form a coalition of stakeholders, including teachers, parents, students, and community members, to support and drive the change process. This coalition can provide diverse perspectives and expertise and help build buy-in and momentum for change. (Leithwood & Louis, 2012).

3. Create a vision for change: Administrators should develop a clear and compelling vision for a more inclusive and equitable learning environment based on research and best practices. This vision should be communicated to all stakeholders, inspiring and motivating them to support the change process. (Fullan, 2011).

4. Communicate the vision: Administrators should communicate the vision for change clearly and consistently to all stakeholders, using a variety of communication methods and channels. Communication methods include newsletters, staff meetings, parent-teacher conferences, and social media. (Kotter, 1996).

5. Empower others to act on the vision: Administrators should empower teachers, students, and other stakeholders to act on the vision for change by providing them with the resources, training, and support necessary to implement new practices and policies. This can include professional development, coaching, and mentoring. (Leithwood & Louis, 2012).

6. Create short-term wins: Administrators should create short-term wins and celebrate successes along the way to build momentum and maintain the commitment of stakeholders. Celebrate success by

recognizing and rewarding individuals and teams that have made significant contributions to the change process. (Kotter, 1996).

7. Consolidate gains and produce more change: Administrators should consolidate the gains that have been made and continue to create more change by building on the successes and lessons learned from the change process. This can involve refining policies and practices, monitoring progress, and adjusting the change plan as needed. (Fullan, 2011).

8. Anchor new approaches in the school culture: Administrators should anchor the new approaches and practices in the school culture by embedding them into the organization's values, norms, and routines. Anchoring the new approaches can involve aligning policies, procedures, and resources with the vision for change and continuously reinforcing the importance of equity and inclusion in education. (Senge, 1990).

Next Steps for Central Office and School Boards

Stepping into the arena to create a more inclusive and equitable learning environment is crucial in shaping the educational landscape of our communities. As decision-makers and policy-makers, Central Office and School Boards hold the power to set the direction for the entire district, impacting countless lives. Embrace your roles as catalysts for positive change and lead the way toward a brighter, more inclusive future where every student can thrive and achieve their dreams. Here are the stages and steps that central office staff and school board of education members can take to create a more inclusive and equitable learning environment:

1. Evaluate:
    a. Create a sense of urgency by identifying and communicating the need for change (Jennings & Rentner, 2016).
    b. Assess the current state of diversity, equity, and inclusion in the school district by collecting data, conducting focus groups or surveys, and engaging with stakeholders (National School Boards Association, 2019).
    c. Identify and challenge the attitudes, beliefs, and behaviors hindering progress toward a more inclusive and equitable learning environment (Lewin, 1951).

2. Transform:
    a. Develop a vision for a more inclusive and equitable learning environment based on research, best practices, and stakeholder input (National School Boards Association, 2019).
    b. Develop and implement strategies and initiatives that promote diversity, equity, and inclusion in education, such as developing policies and practices that promote equal access to resources and opportunities for all students and working to address systemic issues of inequality and injustice (Jennings & Rentner, 2016).
    c. Communicate the vision for change to all stakeholders and engage them in the change process by providing

opportunities for input, feedback, and participation (Lewin, 1951).

3. Strengthen:
   a. Establish new norms, values, and standards that promote equity and inclusion in education and embed these into the school district's culture and practices (Schein, 2010).
   b. Reinforce the new attitudes, beliefs, and behaviors adopted as part of the change process by recognizing and rewarding individuals and teams that have made significant contributions to creating a more inclusive and equitable learning environment (Lewin, 1951).
   c. Celebrate successes and progress made towards the vision for change to maintain momentum and commitment to the change process (National School Boards Association, 2019).

4. Enhancement:
   a. Collect and analyze data on student achievement, engagement, and well-being to evaluate the impact of the change process and make adjustments as needed (Boudreau & Cascio, 2018).
   b. Monitor the implementation of new policies and practices to ensure that they are implemented effectively and consistently across the school district (Jennings & Rentner, 2016).
   c. Provide ongoing support and professional development for school district staff to ensure they have the knowledge and skills to create and sustain an inclusive and equitable

learning environment (National School Boards Association, 2019).

Next Steps for Families and Community Members

Families and community members can play a critical role in advocating for a more inclusive and equitable learning environment. Your involvement in stepping into the arena to create a more inclusive and equitable learning environment is invaluable. As the first and last advocates for our students, your support and dedication can make a significant difference in shaping their educational experiences. Together, let's champion the cause of inclusivity and equity, fostering a nurturing and empowering environment where every child can flourish and realize their full potential. Here are some steps that families and community members can take based on research and best practices:

1. Educate themselves about issues of diversity, equity, and inclusion in education. Families and community members can read books, attend workshops, and engage in dialogue with educators, students, and other stakeholders to deepen their understanding of the challenges and opportunities for creating more inclusive and equitable learning environments (Ladson-Billings & Tate, 2006b).

2. Build relationships with educators, students, and other stakeholders. Families and community members can attend school board meetings, parent-teacher conferences, and other school events to get to know their community's educators, students, and families. This can help build trust, understanding, and collaboration toward

creating a more inclusive and equitable learning environment (Epstein, 2018).

3. Advocate for policies and practices that promote equity and inclusion in education. Families and community members can contact their elected officials, school administrators, and other decision-makers to voice their support for policies and practices that promote equity and inclusion in education. Promoting equity and inclusion can include advocating for increased resources and support for historically marginalized students and pushing for changes to policies and practices that perpetuate inequality and injustice (Losen & Gillespie, 2017).

4. Support and partner with community-based organizations that promote equity and inclusion in education. Support efforts by providing resources, volunteering, and engaging in joint advocacy efforts (Reid & Albee, 1999). Families and community members can collaborate with community-based organizations, such as youth organizations, social justice organizations, and advocacy groups, to support their efforts to create more inclusive and equitable learning environments.

Next Steps for National, State, and Municipal Policymakers

National, State, and Municipal policymakers can also play a critical role in advancing the work toward a more inclusive and equitable learning environment. Stepping into the arena to create a more inclusive and equitable learning environment is a vital responsibility in shaping the future of education. As policymakers, your governance and guidance can drive transformative change, affecting generations of learners. Let us work together to craft a brighter, more inclusive educational landscape that empowers every student, fostering a thriving society built on equal opportunities and shared success. Here are a few steps that policymakers can take based on research and best practices:

1. Promote policies and practices that address systemic issues of inequality and injustice in education. Policymakers can use their influence to promote policies and practices that support every student's academic success and well-being, particularly those from historically marginalized communities. This can include policies related to funding, teacher training, curriculum development, and student support services (National Equity Project, 2018b).

2. Engage with educators, students, and community members to understand the challenges and opportunities for creating more inclusive and equitable learning environments. Policymakers can hold public hearings, conduct site visits, and engage in dialogue with stakeholders to deepen their understanding of the issues and build support for policy solutions (Darling-Hammond, 2017).

3. Support research and evaluation to inform policy decisions related to equity and inclusion in education. Policymakers can support research studies and evaluations that help to identify effective practices and policies for creating more inclusive and equitable learning environments and use this information to guide policy decisions (National Education Policy Center, 2019).

4. Build coalitions and partnerships with other policymakers, advocates, and organizations to advance policies that promote equity and inclusion in education. Policymakers can collaborate with other stakeholders to build support for policy solutions and amplify the voices of those most affected by inequity and injustice in education (Khalifa & Gooden, 2016).

Hopefully, through the research presented, the stories and experiences shared, and deep personal reflection, this book has provided insight into our students' adversities and a better understanding of what we can do. So, my fellow travelers on this equitable and just education journey for all, let us embrace vulnerability, practice self-compassion, and lean on one another as we courageously take those first steps into the arena. May we step into the arena knowing that our strength lies not in the absence of fear but our willingness to face it head-on. We are the champions that our students need, not yesterday, not tomorrow, but today. May we begin to all work together to lighten the load our students carry in their backpacks.

Am I willing to face potential criticism, rejection, or backlash in order to stand up for what I believe is right?

Stories matter

Voices of Marginalized Students

Overcoming Adversity

The stories of this bonus chapter were shared with me by a few individuals who wanted to share their experiences as marginalized students. I know some of the individuals in these stories well, and some I know indirectly through online sources. The stories were added with minor edits, such as occasional misspelled words, punctuations, and paragraphs. I did my best to keep them as they were originally shared. Names were changed or omitted to protect the identity of individuals who were part of the story but may not want their names associated. The stories were shared in good faith that they were all true. Thank you to the storytellers for having the courage to share.

A Child of Two Different Worlds

"There was a time when I wished others knew how difficult it was for me to navigate between two different worlds as a child of immigrant parents. I felt the constant pressure to blend in with my classmates at school while simultaneously honoring my family's cultural roots. It often felt like walking a tightrope, trying to maintain a delicate balance.

At school, I was surrounded by peers who spoke English effortlessly and seemed to have a shared understanding of the culture. I envied their ease and desperately wanted to be like them. I tried to mimic their accents, clothing, and mannerisms, hoping to fit in and be accepted. But the moment I got home, I found myself in a completely different world, where my parents insisted that I maintain our cultural traditions and speak our native language. This dual identity left me feeling isolated, unable to fit in completely in either place.

I wanted my teacher to understand my struggles, but I was too scared to share them. I worried that admitting my difficulties would make me seem weak, or worse, that my teacher would think I wasn't trying hard enough. In reality, I was giving my all, but it felt like I was always coming up short. I longed for my teacher to see the person behind the facade, to recognize the challenges I faced, and to offer support and understanding."

-Susana, 36, Social Worker

Suffering in Silence

"Growing up as a gay Latino, I never imagined that there would be a time when I would dread going to school. I always enjoyed learning, and school had been a place where I felt safe and supported. But all that changed when the bullying started. I couldn't understand why my classmates targeted me, making me feel like I didn't belong simply because of who I was.

At first, the taunts and mockery seemed harmless, but as time passed, they became more vicious and personal. The bullies ridiculed my ethnicity, accent, and sexuality, making it impossible for me to find solace in the once familiar school environment. I was afraid to be myself, worried that even the smallest expression of my identity would draw more attention and further torment.

I desperately wished people knew the anguish I experienced every day. I wanted them to see the hurt in my eyes and understand the weight of the burden I carried. I longed for them support, for them to intervene and help create a safe space where I could be myself without fear. But I was afraid. Afraid that revealing my pain would only make things worse.

As the days turned into weeks, and the weeks into months, I continued to suffer in silence. I wished more than anything that people could see through my mask of stoicism and recognize the turmoil beneath. I needed someone to stand up for me, to let me know that I was not alone, and that it was okay to be a gay Latino in a world that sometimes felt so unwelcoming."

-James, 26, Social Media Manager

173

I Just Needed Support

"During my high school years, I faced a situation I never thought I'd experience - homelessness. I felt a constant, gnawing anxiety as I struggled to find a quiet place to do my homework and worried about where I would sleep each night. Despite my best efforts, focusing on schoolwork was nearly impossible with such pressing concerns.

I wished that my principal and teachers knew about my circumstances, but I was too embarrassed and afraid to reveal my secret. I knew I needed help, but I didn't want to be pitied or treated differently from my classmates. So, I kept my head down and continued to do my best, hoping that one day, things would get better.

One afternoon, when I thought no one was around, I broke down in tears in an empty classroom, feeling utterly overwhelmed. To my surprise, my principal walked in, concern etched on her face. I hesitated, but eventually opened up about my situation. She listened with empathy and reassured me that I wasn't alone.

My principal took action and connected me with resources that made a significant difference. She arranged for me to have access to the school library after hours so I could complete my homework in a quiet, safe environment. She also connected my family with a local organization that provided temporary housing and support services, giving us a chance to get back on our feet.

Over time, my life began to stabilize, and I could finally concentrate on my studies without the constant fear and worry. With the help of my principal and the support of my school, I graduated with honors and earned a scholarship to college. I'll always be grateful for the compassion and understanding that transformed my life, turning a time of despair into a story of hope and resilience."

-Yennie, 33, Accountant

Invisible Struggle

"During my teen years I felt like I was trapped in a never-ending battle with my own mind. I struggled with depression and anxiety, and the weight of these emotions made it difficult for me to find the energy and motivation to face each day. Sometimes, just getting out of bed in the morning felt like an insurmountable challenge, let alone focusing in class and participating in activities.

I wished my teachers could see the invisible struggle I faced every day. I wanted them to understand that my lack of engagement wasn't because I didn't care about my education or that I was lazy, but because my mental health was making it nearly impossible for me to function. However, I didn't feel comfortable enough to share my struggle, fearing that someone might think less of me or that I was just making excuses.

As the weeks wore on, my academic performance began to suffer, and I could see the disappointment in my teachers' eyes. I felt helpless and ashamed, believing that I was letting them down. One day, after class, one teacher pulled me aside and asked if everything was okay. She expressed genuine concern for me and offered a listening ear, giving me the courage to finally open up about my depression and anxiety.

My teacher's understanding and support made all the difference. She helped me develop strategies to manage my workload and offered accommodations to ensure I had the opportunity to succeed. With her encouragement, I also sought professional help, which helped me gain control of my mental health.

Looking back, I am grateful that my teacher saw past my struggles and offered me the support and empathy I needed. It was the turning point that allowed me to overcome my challenges and succeed not only in school but in life as well."

-Rashod, 41, Technical Support Manager

Defense Mechanism

"Growing up as a foster child, I felt like I was always on the move, never staying in one place long enough to build a stable life. Over the years, I had been in and out of countless homes, each time facing the daunting task of adjusting to new surroundings and trying to fit in. It seemed as though just when I started to feel comfortable, I was uprooted again, leaving any semblance of stability behind.

I wanted my teachers to know about my situation, but I was determined to make it on my own, without anyone's help or pity. I kept my secret, convinced that I could overcome the challenges I faced as a foster child. My defense mechanism was to avoid getting too close to people, making it easier to leave when the time came. This made it incredibly difficult to trust anyone, let alone make friends.

As the months passed, I became an expert at blending into the background, navigating my way through school without drawing attention to myself. I studied hard, seeking solace in my academic achievements, and took pride in my independence. I wanted to prove that I could make it on my own, despite the obstacles life had thrown my way.

Though my journey was tough and at times lonely, it taught me resilience and strength. I learned that even in the face of uncertainty and constant change, I could persevere and succeed. In the end, I graduated with honors, a testament to my determination and hard work.

Looking back, I realize that my experiences as a foster child shaped me into the person I am today. While I chose to face my challenges alone, I now understand the importance of allowing others in and embracing the support they offer. I am proud of what I accomplished on my own, but I also know that it's okay to lean on others when we need help."

-Matthew, 27, Retail Manager

I Just Wanted Your Help

"When I was in school, there was a time when I really wished my teacher knew that I wanted to do well in his class, but math was tough for me. I tried my best, but no matter how hard I worked, I just couldn't get the hang of it. I wanted to ask my teacher for help, but every time I did, he would talk down to me, making me feel bad about myself.

Because of this, I started looking for help from other people. I would spend hours with friends, family, and even tutors who were kind enough to help me understand the math problems I was struggling with. It was a lot of hard work, but I was determined to do well and not let my math troubles hold me back.

Eventually, all that hard work paid off, and I was able to get through my math classes. As I got older, I discovered that I was really good at helping people and had a talent for working with my hands. So, I decided to become a dental hygienist, a job that would let me use those skills to help people take care of their teeth and have healthy smiles. What was once hidden from me, I was able to help give to others.

Looking back, I am proud that I didn't let my math struggles or my teacher's attitude stop me from reaching my goals. I learned that even if something is difficult, with determination and the right support, I could overcome any obstacle. And now, as a dental hygienist, I get to help people every day, which makes me feel really good about what I've accomplished."

-Cynthia, 27, Dental Hygienist

Finding My Place

"When I was in school, I often felt misunderstood by the staff. They saw me as a white kid and assumed that I had all the privileges that came with it. But they didn't know that my reality was far from it. I grew up in a poor family, the youngest of five siblings, and my parents didn't know English. I never wanted to cause trouble, but I struggled to find my place, and sometimes that led to me making mistakes.

I wished the staff at school could see beyond the color of my skin and understand that I faced my own set of challenges. I wanted them to know that I was trying my best, but it wasn't easy navigating a world where my parents couldn't communicate with my teachers, and I had to figure things out on my own.

As the years went by, I worked hard to overcome these obstacles. I studied diligently and learned to adapt to the expectations of my school and society. I also took on part-time jobs to help support my family, gradually developing a strong work ethic and a keen sense of responsibility.

After high school, I became increasingly interested in real estate. I educated myself on the ins and outs of the industry and started investing in properties. Over time, my investments grew, and I became a successful real estate investor. I was able to provide a comfortable life for my family and even teach my parents English, bridging the communication gap that had been a constant challenge for us.

Looking back, I am grateful for the hardships I faced because they made me stronger and more resilient. I am proud of what I have achieved, and I now use my success to give back to my community and help others who face similar challenges. I learned that with determination and hard work, it is possible to overcome any obstacle and build a better life for ourselves and our families. As an adult I also learned that it did not need to be that hard for us with the right help and support."

-Simon, 51, Business Owner

Breaking the Cycle

"Growing up, my brother and I faced many challenges, but none as difficult as his addiction to drugs during high school. It was a dark and painful time for our family, and we felt helpless as we watched him spiral deeper into his addiction. Thankfully, his guidance counselor, Mr. Thompson, saw the potential in my brother and tried his best to help him.

Mr. Thompson went above and beyond, meeting with my brother regularly and offering support and encouragement. He connected him with resources and even stayed late after school to provide a safe space for him to open up about his struggles. But my brother, blinded by his addiction, refused to accept Mr. Thompson's help, convinced that he could handle everything on his own.

Tragically, my brother was later diagnosed with cancer. As his health deteriorated, we spent many hours by his bedside, sharing memories and offering comfort. During one of our conversations, he tearfully admitted how much he regretted not accepting Mr. Thompson's help. He realized that the guidance counselor had genuinely cared for him and tried to save him from a dangerous path, but he had been too stubborn to listen.

As I grieved the loss of my brother, I found solace in the lessons he had shared with me. I was determined not to make the same mistakes he had, and I sought Mr. Thompson's guidance. He helped me break free from the cycle of substance abuse and incarceration that had ensnared my brother, and for that, I am eternally grateful.

My brother's life was a painful reminder of the consequences of addiction and the importance of accepting help when it is offered. Though Mr. Thompson couldn't save my brother, his efforts did not go in vain. He saved me, and in doing so, he changed the course of my life. I will always remember him as the guiding light that pulled me from the darkness and set me on a path toward a brighter future."

-Timothy, 37, Senior Marketing Manager

Being the change is not just a choice, but a responsibility we bear as citizens of the world, for it is through our actions and hearts that we can create a future filled with promise and possibility.

About The Author

Dr. Edwin Garcia, Jr. is an urban school educator in New Jersey. He holds a master's degree in Educational Technology and another master's degree in Educational Leadership. He also holds a doctorate in Curriculum and Instruction. Dr. Garcia started his career as Middle School Business Teacher and then as a Secondary Education Computer Science Teacher in the district where he was once a student himself. He later became an Assistant Principal at a comprehensive high school with over 2,500 students. As a High School Assistant Principal, Dr. Garcia oversaw Business Education, Career and Technical Education, Math, and Science departments. He has also been the lead facilitator for the school testing and data teams. Additionally, Dr. Garcia has been the facilitator for Dual Enrollment, Advance Placement, and Student Career Certification programs. He is most proud of the work he co-led to revise and implement the school's remedial and disciplinary measures, including robust restitution and restoration practices. Dr. Garcia is passionate about speaking his truth and bringing equitable education opportunities for **ALL STUDENTS.**

f **DrGarciaEdu**
in **DrGarciaEdu**
🐦 **DrGarciaEdu**

JUST RISE ED
TRANSFORMING EDUCATION
www.JustRiseEd.com
DrEdwinGarciaJr@justriseed.com

References

Allport, G. W., Clark, K., & Pettigrew, T. (1954). *The nature of prejudice.*

American Psychological Association. (2018). *School discipline and the school-to-prison pipeline.* https://www.apa.org/advocacy/criminal-justice/school-to-prison-pipeline

Anda, R. F., Felitti, V. J., Bremner, J. D., Walker, J. D., Whitfield, C. H., Perry, B. D., ... & Giles, W. H. (2006). The enduring effects of abuse and related adverse experiences in childhood: A convergence of evidence from neurobiology and epidemiology. *European Archives of Psychiatry and clinical neuroscience,* 256(3), 174–186.

Baker, J. A., Grant, S., & Morlock, L. (2008). The teacher-student relationship as a developmental context for children with internalizing or externalizing behavior problems. *School Psychology Quarterly*, 23(1), 3–15.

Bandura, A. (1977). Self-efficacy: Toward a unifying theory of behavioral change. *Psychological Review*, 84(2), 191–215.

Bandura, A. (1993). Perceived self-efficacy in cognitive development and functioning. *Educational Psychologist*, 28(2), 117–148.

Bastian, K. C., & Chen, Y. (2016). Alternative certification programs and the diversity of the teacher workforce. *Education and Urban Society*, 48(5), 429-451.

Beets, M. W., Weaver, R. G., Turner-McGrievy, G., Huberty, J., Moore, J. B., Ward, D. S., & Freedman, D. A. (2014). Making the case for comprehensive school physical activity programs: An overview of systematic reviews. *Preventive medicine*, p. 69, S3-S12.

Bell, A. D., & Lederman, R. (2020). Creating an inclusive classroom culture: A guide to transformative teaching. *Stylus Publishing*, LLC.

Berk, R. A. (2004). *Professors are from Mars, students are from Snickers: How to write and deliver humor in the classroom and in professional presentations.* Stylus Publishing, LLC.

Best, P., Manktelow, R., & Taylor, B. (2014). Online communication, social media and adolescent wellbeing: A systematic narrative review. *Children and Youth Services Review*, 41, 27-36.

Bettinger, E., & Baker, R. (2011). *The Effects of Student Coaching in College: An Evaluation of a Randomized Experiment in Student Mentoring*. NBER Working Paper No. 16881. National Bureau of Economic Research.

Black, P., & Wiliam, D. (1998). Assessment and classroom learning. *Assessment in Education: Principles, Policy & Practice*, 5(1), 7–74.

Blackwell, L. S., Trzesniewski, K. H., & Dweck, C. S. (2007). Implicit theories of intelligence predict achievement across an adolescent transition: A longitudinal study and an intervention. *Child Development*, 78(1), 246-263. https://doi.org/10.1111/j.1467-8624.2007.00995.x

Blair, I. V. (2002). The malleability of automatic stereotypes and prejudice. *Personality and Social Psychology Review*, 6(3), 242–261. doi:10.1207/S15327957PSPR0603_8

Bloom, J. (2019). Generation activism: How young activists are changing the world. *The Guardian*. Retrieved from https://www.theguardian.com/lifeandstyle/2019/sep/09/generation-activism-how-young-activists-are-changing-the-world

Borman, G. D., & Dowling, N. M. (2010). Teacher expectations and student achievement: A meta-analysis. *Journal of Educational Research*, 102(1), 47–65. https://doi.org/10.1080/00220670903383033

Boudreau, J. W., & Cascio, W. F. (2018). Leading the transformation: Applying agile and devops principles at scale. *Harvard Business Press*.

Brackett, M. A., Reyes, M. R., Rivers, S. E., Elbertson, N. A., & Salovey, P. (2011). Classroom emotional climate, teacher affiliation, and student conduct. *The Journal of classroom interaction*, pp. 27–36.

Brookhart, S. M. (2013). Letter grades: A minus or D plus? *Educational Leadership*, 70(1), 16–20.

References

Brown, B. (2012). *Daring greatly: How the courage to be vulnerable transforms the way we live, love, parent, and lead.* Penguin.

Burnette, J. L., O'Boyle, E. H., VanEpps, E. M., Pollack, J. M., & Finkel, E. J. (2013). Mind-sets matter: A meta-analytic review of implicit theories and self-regulation. *Psychological Bulletin*, 139(3), 655–701.

Cassady, J. C., & Johnson, R. E. (2002). Cognitive test anxiety and academic performance. *Contemporary Educational Psychology*, 27(2), 270–295. https://doi.org/10.1006/ceps.2001.1094

Center for American Progress. (2019). *The state of diversity in today's educator workforce.* https://www.americanprogress.org/issues/education-k-12/reports/2019/09/17/474928/state-diversity-todays-educator-workforce/

Cohen, J. (2018). *Zero grades: What are they good for?* Phi Delta Kappan, 99(5), 68-72.

Cohen, G. L., & Garcia, J. (2008). Identity, belonging, and achievement: A model, interventions, implications. *Current Directions in Psychological Science*, 17(6), 365-369. doi: 10.1111/j.1467-8721.2008.00590.x

Cohen, G. L., Garcia, J., Apfel, N., & Master, A. (2006). Reducing the racial achievement gap: A social-psychological intervention. *Science*, 313(5791), 1307-1310.

Cohen, J., McCabe, E. M., Michelli, N. M., & Pickeral, T. (2009). School climate: Research, policy, practice, and teacher education. *Teachers college record*, 111(1), 180–213.

Cokley, K. O., Awad, G. H., Smith, L., Jackson, S., Awosogba, O., Hurst, A., & Roberts, D. (2018). A review of the application and impact of multicultural competencies in psychology training. *The Counseling Psychologist*, 46(5), 636–658. doi: 10.1177/0011000018782535

Cornelius-White, J. (2007). Learner-centered teacher-student relationships are effective: A meta-analysis. *Review of Educational Research*, 77(1), 113–143.

Covington, M. V. (2000). Goal theory, motivation, and school achievement: An integrative review. *Annual Review of Psychology*, 51(1), 171–200.

Croninger, R. G., & Lee, V. E. (2001). Social capital and dropping out of high school: Benefits to at-risk students of teachers' support and guidance. *Teachers College Record*, 103(4), 548-581.

Cross, M. B., Kim, Y., & Vance, L. A. (2018). Trauma-informed schools: Building safe and nurturing learning environments for all children. *Children & Schools*, 40(4), 213–220.

Darling-Hammond, L. (2017). Teacher education around the world: What can we learn from international practice? *European Journal of Teacher Education*, 40(3), 291–309.

Darling-Hammond, L., Flook, L., Cook-Harvey, C., Barron, B., & Osher, D. (2020). Implications for educational practice of the science of learning and development. *Applied Developmental Science*, 24(2), 97–140. https://doi.org/10.1080/10888691.2018.1537791

Darling-Hammond, L., Hyler, M. E., & Gardner, M. (2017). *Effective teacher diversity: Models and promising practices.* Palo Alto, CA: Learning Policy Institute.

Deci, E. L., & Ryan, R. M. (2000). The "what" and "why" of goal pursuits: Human needs and the self-determination of behavior. *Psychological Inquiry*, 11(4), 227–268.

Deci, E. L., Koestner, R., & Ryan, R. M. (2001). Extrinsic rewards and intrinsic motivation in education: Reconsidered once again. *Review of educational research*, 71(1), 1-27.

Dee, T. S. (2004). Teachers, race, and student achievement in a randomized experiment. *The Review of Economics and Statistics*, 86(1), 195–210.

Denny, G. S., & Lo, W. J. (2009). A study of psychological distress among African American, Asian American, and Latino college students. *Cultural Diversity and Ethnic Minority Psychology*, 15(1), 49-55. https://doi.org/10.1037/a0013262

Devine, P. G., Forscher, P. S., Austin, A. J., & Cox, W. T. (2012). Long-term reduction in implicit race bias: A prejudice habit-breaking intervention. *Journal of Experimental Social Psychology*, 48(6), 1267-1278.

References

Duncan, G. J., & Magnuson, K. (2013). *The long reach of early childhood poverty.* Economic stress, human capital, and families in Asia: Research and policy challenges, pp. 57–70.

Durlak, J. A., Weissberg, R. P., Dymnicki, A. B., Taylor, R. D., & Schellinger, K. B. (2011). The impact of enhancing students' social and emotional learning: A meta-analysis of school-based universal interventions. *Child Development*, 82(1), 405-432.

Dweck, C. S. (2006). *Mindset: The new psychology of success.* Random House.

Dweck, C. S. (2015). Carol Dweck revisits the 'growth mindset'. *Education Week*, 35(5), 20–24.

Eccles, J. S., & Roeser, R. W. (2011). Schools, academic motivation, and stage-environment fit. *In Handbook of Adolescent Psychology* (pp. 404–434). Wiley. https://doi.org/10.1002/9781118018232

Eccles, J. S., & Wigfield, A. (2002). Motivational beliefs, values, and goals. *Annual Review of Psychology*, pp. 53, 109–132. doi: 10.1146/annurev.psych.53.100901.135153

Eisenberg, N., & Miller, P. A. (1987). Empathy, sympathy, and altruism: Empirical and conceptual links. In N. Eisenberg & J. Strayer (Eds.), *Empathy and its development* (pp. 292-316). Cambridge University Press.

Elias, M. J., & Langer, J. (2017). *Promoting social and emotional learning: Guidelines for educators.* Alexandria, VA: ASCD.

Epstein, J. L. (2018). *School, family, and community partnerships: Preparing educators and improving schools.* Routledge.

Feldman, J. (2019). *Grading for Equity: What It Is, Why It Matters, and How It Can Transform Schools and Classrooms.* Corwin Press.

Ferguson, R. (2010). Can schools narrow the black-white test score gap? *Education Next*, 10(1), 72–78.

Ferguson, R. F. (2019). The education of students of color and students of low socioeconomic status. *Future of Children*, 29(2), 15–32. https://www.jstor.org/stable/26895398

Fredricks, J. A., Blumenfeld, P. C., & Paris, A. H. (2004). School engagement: Potential of the concept, state of the evidence. *Review of Educational Research*, 74(1), 59-109.

Fuligni, A. J., Tu, J. J., Yip, T., & Lam, M. (2019). Fostering excellence: Teachers' expectations and sense of responsibility for students' academic achievement. *Journal of Educational Psychology*, 111(3), 488-505.

Fullan, M. (2011). *Change leader: Learning to do what matters most.* John Wiley & Sons.

Garg, A., Butz, A. M., Dworkin, P. H., Lewis, R. A., Thompson, R. E., & Serwint, J. R. (2018). Improving the management of family psychosocial problems at low-income children's well-child care visits: The WE CARE Project. *Pediatrics*, 121(2), 547–555.

Gay, G. (2010). *Culturally responsive teaching: Theory, research, and practice.* New York: Teachers College Press.

Gay, G. (2002). Preparing for culturally responsive teaching. *Journal of Teacher Education*, 53(2), 106–116.

Gay, G. (2018*). Culturally responsive teaching: Theory, research, and practice (3rd ed.).* New York, NY: Teachers College Press.

Gehlbach, H., Brinkworth, M. E., & Harris, A. D. (2016). Changes in teacher–student relationships. *In Handbook of Social and Emotional Learning: Research and Practice* (pp. 194-207). Guilford Publications.

Gershenson, S., Holt, S. B., & Papageorge, N. W. (2017). Who believes in me? The effect of student–teacher demographic match on teacher expectations. *Economics of Education Review*, 64, 70-89.

Gersten, R., Baker, S. K., Shanahan, T., Linan-Thompson, S., & Collins, P. (2006). *Effective literacy and English language instruction for English learners in the elementary grades: A practice guide (NCEE 2007-4011).* Washington, DC: National Center for Education Evaluation and Regional Assistance, Institute of Education Sciences, U.S. Department of Education.

References

Gillies, R. M., & Boyle, M. (2010). Teachers' reflections on cooperative learning: Issues of implementation. *Teaching and Teacher Education*, 26(4), 933–940.

Ginsburg, K. R. (2017). The importance of having high expectations for children and youth with disabilities. *Exceptional Parent*, 47(10), 26–30.

Ginwright, S. (2018). *Just Schools: A Whole School Approach to Restorative Justice.* Teachers College Press.

GAO. (2018). *K-12 Education: Discipline Disparities for Black Students, Boys, and Students with Disabilities.* Government Accountability Office.

Golberstein, E., Wen, H., & Miller, B. F. (2021). Coronavirus disease 2019 (COVID-19) and mental health for children and adolescents. *JAMA pediatrics*, 175(9), 817-818.

Good, C., Aronson, J., & Inzlicht, M. (2012). Improving adolescents' standardized test performance: An intervention to reduce the effects of stereotype threat. *Journal of Applied Developmental Psychology*, 33(3), 136-143.

Goodenow, C. (1993). Classroom belonging among early adolescent students: Relationships to motivation and achievement. *The Journal of early adolescence*, 13(1), 21–43.

Gorski, P. (2017). *Reaching and Teaching Students in Poverty: Strategies for Erasing the Opportunity Gap.* United Kingdom: Teachers College Press, Teachers College, Columbia University.

Gorski, P. C. (2018). Equity literacy for all. *Educational Leadership*, 76(3), 50-55.

Gregory, A., Clawson, K., Davis, A., & Gerewitz, J. (2016). Moving Beyond Punitive Discipline: Restorative Practices in Schools. *Youth Justice*, 16(2), 99–119. https://doi.org/10.1177/1473225416639474

Hammond, Z. (2015). *Culturally responsive teaching and the brain: Promoting authentic engagement and rigor among culturally and linguistically diverse students.* Corwin Press.

Hamre, B. K., & Pianta, R. C. (2001). Early teacher-child relationships and the trajectory of children's school outcomes through eighth grade. *Child Development*, 72(2), 625-638.

Harrison, C. (2019). *Setting realistic expectations for students*. The University of Texas at Austin College of Education. https://education.utexas.edu/news/2019/10/01/setting-realistic-expectations-students

Hattie, J. (2012). *Visible learning for teachers: Maximizing impact on learning*. Routledge.

Hattie, J., & Timperley, H. (2007). The power of feedback. *Review of Educational Research*, 77(1), 81–112. doi:10.3102/003465430298487

Hoyt, C. L., & Blascovich, J. (2010). The collective face of stereotype threat: A meta-analysis on collective efficacy and stereotype threat. *Journal of Applied Psychology*, 95(5), 728-744. doi: 10.1037/a0020250

Hughes, J. N., Cavell, T. A., & Willson, V. (2001). Further support for the developmental significance of the quality of the teacher-student relationship. *Journal of School Psychology*, 39(4), 289–301.

Hughes, J. N., Luo, W., Kwok, O. M., & Loyd, L. K. (2008). Teacher-Student Support, Effortful Engagement, and Achievement: A 3-Year Longitudinal Study. *Journal of educational psychology*, *100*(1), 1–14. https://doi.org/10.1037/0022-0663.100.1.1

Hulleman, C. S., Schrager, S. M., Bodmann, S. M., & Harackiewicz, J. M. (2010). A meta-analytic review of achievement goal measures: Different labels for the same constructs or different constructs with similar labels? *Psychological Bulletin*, 136(3), 422-449. http://dx.doi.org/10.1037/a0018947

Järvelä, S., Järvenoja, H., Malmberg, J., Isohätälä, J., & Sobocinski, M. (2016). How do types of interaction and phases of self-regulated learning set a stage for collaborative engagement? *Learning and Instruction*, 43, 39-51.

Jennings, J., & Rentner, D. S. (2016). *Improving equity and access: The second in a series of three briefs on the ESSA evidence standards*. Learning Policy Institute.

Jennings, P. A., & Greenberg, M. T. (2009). The prosocial classroom: Teacher social and emotional competence in relation to student and classroom outcomes. *Review of Educational Research*, 79(1), 491–525.

References

Jussim, L., & Harber, K. D. (2005). Teacher expectations and self-fulfilling prophecies: Knowns and unknowns, resolved and unresolved controversies. *Personality and Social Psychology Review*, 9(2), 131-155.

Kahan, J. P. (1996). *Punishment in Search of a Crime: Americans and the Necessity of Law and Order.* Oxford University Press.

Kafele, B. (2013). *Closing the attitude gap: How to fire up your students to strive for success.* ASCD.

Kataoka, S. H., Stein, B. D., Jaycox, L. H., Wong, M., Escudero, P., Tu, W., & Zaragoza, C. (2013). A school-based mental health program for traumatized Latino immigrant children. *Journal of the American Academy of Child & Adolescent Psychiatry*, 52(8), 853-862.

Khalifa, M., & Gooden, M. A. (2016). Culturally responsive school leadership: A synthesis of the literature. *Review of Educational Research*, 86(4), 1272–1311.

Kim, J., & Bayne, L. (2019). Culturally responsive teaching and the strengths perspective: A framework for student success. *Journal of Ethnic and Cultural Diversity in Social Work*, 28(2), 97-114. doi: 10.1080/15313204.2018.1518637

Kim, J. E., & Hwang, J. Y. (2018). A qualitative study of low-income students' experiences in higher education: Navigating social and academic challenges. *College Student Journal*, 52(2), 239-252.

Kostelnik, B., Stein, D., Whelan, J., Pinkard, N., & Winokur, J. (2016). Building trauma-informed schools and communities. *Educational Leadership*, 73(6), 56-60.

Kotter, J. P. (1996). *Leading change.* Harvard Business Press.

Kozol, J. (2012). *Savage inequalities: Children in America's schools.* Broadway Books.

Krezmien, M. P., Leone, P. E., & Achilles, G. M. (2006). Suspension, Race, and Disability: Analysis of Statewide Practices and Reporting. *Journal of Emotional and Behavioral Disorders*, 14(4), 217–226. https://doi.org/10.1177/10634266060140040201

Ladson-Billings, G. (1995). Toward a theory of culturally relevant pedagogy. *American Educational Research Journal*, 32(3), 465-491.

Ladson-Billings, G. (2006). From the achievement gap to the education debt: Understanding achievement in U.S. schools. *Educational Researcher*, 35(7), 3-12.

Ladson-Billings, G. (2019). *Culturally Relevant Pedagogy 2.0: A.K.A. the Remix.* Harvard Educational Review, 89(1), 1-24.

Ladson-Billings, G., & Tate, W. F. (2006a). *Education research in the public interest: Social justice, action, and policy.* Teachers College Press.

Ladson-Billings, G., & Tate, W. F. (2006b). Toward a critical race theory of education. *Teachers College Record*, 108(6), 923-946.

Lee, J. (2020). Preparing mainstream teachers for English language learners: A review of the research. *Teaching and Teacher Education*, p. 88, 102957.

Lee, O., & Bowen, N. K. (2006). Cultural competence and teacher preparation: A conceptual synthesis. *Theory Into Practice*, 45(3), 173–183.

Leithwood, K., & Louis, K. S. (2012). *Linking leadership to student learning.* John Wiley & Sons.

Lewin, K. (1951). *Field theory in social science: Selected theoretical papers.* Harper & Row.

Lindsay, G., & Hart, A. (2017). A systematic review of the relationship between teacher expectations and student achievement. *Educational Psychology Review*, 29(4), 653–690. https://doi.org/10.1007/s10648-016-9391-3

Lindsey, R. B., Roberts, L. M., & Campbell Jones, L. (2013). *The culturally proficient school: An implementation guide for school leaders.* Corwin Press.

Lindsey, R. B., Roberts, L. M., & Campbell-Jones, F. (2018). *The culturally responsive educator.* Corwin Press.

Linley, P. A., & Harrington, S. (2006). Playing to your strengths. *The Psychologist*, 19(2), 86–89.

Locke, E. A., & Latham, G. P. (2002). Building a practically useful theory of goal setting and task motivation: A 35-year odyssey. *American Psychologist*, 57(9), 705–717.

References

Loeb, S., & Reininger, M. (2004). How much are teachers using data to improve instruction? *Educational Evaluation and Policy Analysis*, 26(4), 331-349. doi:10.3102/01623737026004331

Lopes, P. N., Salovey, P., & Straus, R. (2011). Emotional intelligence, personality, and the perceived quality of social relationships. *Personality and Individual Differences*, 51(2), 156–161.

Losen, D. J., & Gillespie, J. (2012). *Opportunities suspended: The devastating consequences of zero tolerance and school discipline policies*. The Civil Rights Project, UCLA.

Losen, D. J., & Gillespie, J. (2017). *Opportunities suspended: The disparate impact of disciplinary exclusion from school.* UCLA Civil Rights Project.

Losen, D. J., & Skiba, R. J. (2010). Suspended Education: Urban Middle Schools in Crisis. *The Journal of Negro Education*, 79(3), 330–343. https://doi.org/10.7709/jnegroeducation.79.3.0330

Mallette, L. A., & Ruiz, N. M. (2017). *The impact of teacher expectations on students of color.* In S. R. Harper & S. J. Quaye (Eds.), Student engagement in higher education: Theoretical perspectives and practical approaches for diverse populations (pp. 219-237). Routledge.

Manca, S., & Ranieri, M. (2016). "Yes for sharing, no for teaching!": Social Media in academic practices. *The Internet and Higher Education*, 29, 63-74.

Marzano, R. J., Marzano, J. S., & Pickering, D. J. (2003). *Classroom management that works: Research-based strategies for every teacher.* ASCD.

Marzano, R. J., & Kendall, J. S. (2007). *The new taxonomy of educational objectives (2nd ed.).* Corwin Press.

McKown, C., & Weinstein, R. S. (2018). Teacher biases against the socioeconomically disadvantaged: The role of school organizational structure. *Journal of Educational Psychology*, 110(7), 916-929.

Melnick, H., & Martinez, L. (2018). *Strategies for building a supportive and inclusive school climate.* Learning Policy Institute.

Mendoza, M. A., & Reese, L. (2018). Cultural mismatch theory: Revisiting cultural discontinuity and the education of Black and Latino children. *Journal of Negro Education*, 87(3), 225-238. doi: 10.7709/jnee.87.3.0225

Milner, H. R., & Howard, T. C. (2018). African American teachers' perspectives on culturally relevant teaching: A narrative inquiry. *Urban Education*, 53(6), 694–711.

Molina, L. E., & Starr, L. M. (2020). Asset-based education: Promoting student strengths and success. *Journal of Adolescent Health*, 66(3S), S26-S31.

Monteith, M. J., Ashburn-Nardo, L., Voils, C. I., & Czopp, A. M. (2002). Putting the brakes on prejudice: On the development and operation of cues for control. *Journal of Personality and Social Psychology*, 83(5), 1029–1050. doi:10.1037/0022-3514.83.5.1029

Morris, M. (2016). *Pushout: The Criminalization of Black Girls in Schools.* The New Press.

Murray, C., & Malmgren, K. (2005). Implementing a teacher-student relationship program in a high-poverty urban school: Effects on social, emotional, and academic adjustment and lessons learned. *Journal of School Psychology*, 43(2), 137–152. https://doi.org/10.1016/j.jsp.2005.01.003

National Academies of Sciences, Engineering, and Medicine. 2019. *A Roadmap to Reducing Child Poverty.* Washington, DC: The National Academies Press. https://doi.org/10.17226/25246.

National Academy for State Health Policy. (2019). *Strengthening the School-Based Health Center Workforce: A State Survey.* Author.

National Association of Community Health Centers. (2013). *School-based health centers: National census school year 2011-2012.* Author.

National Center for Education Statistics. (2021). *The condition of education: Racial/ethnic and socioeconomic disparities in academic achievement.* U.S. Department of Education.

References

National Child Traumatic Stress Network. (n.d.). *The essential elements of a trauma-informed school.* Retrieved from https://www.nctsn.org/sites/default/files/resources/essential_elements_of_a_trauma-informed_school.pdf

National Conference of State Legislatures. (2018). *School-based health centers.* Author.

National Council on Teacher Quality (NCTQ). (2020). *Increasing teacher diversity: Strategies to improve the teacher workforce.* Retrieved from https://www.nctq.org/dmsView/Increasing_Teacher_Diversity_Strategies_to_Improve_the_Teacher_Workforce_NCTQ_Report

National Education Association. (2015). *Cultural competence in the classroom.* https://www.nea.org/advocating-for-change/new-from-nea/cultural-competence-classroom

National Education Policy Center. (2019). *Equity and education.* Retrieved from https://nepc.colorado.edu/topic/equity-and-education

National Equity Project. (2018a). *Equity by Design: How UDL and Culturally Responsive Teaching Can Work Together.* http://nationalequityproject.org/wp-content/uploads/2018/05/Equity-by-Design-UDL-CRT.pdf

National Equity Project. (2018b). *The 8 principles of equity-centered leadership.* Retrieved from https://nationalequityproject.org/8-principles-equity-centered-leadership

National Equity Project. (2019). *Educational equity: What is it and why does it matter?* Retrieved from https://www.nationalequityproject.org/educational-equity-what-is-it-and-why-does-it-matter/

National School Boards Association. (2019). *Leading the way to equity: Advancing opportunities for all students.*

Neff, K. (2011). *Self-compassion: The proven power of being kind to yourself.* HarperCollins.

Neff, K. D., & Vonk, R. (2009). Self-compassion versus global self-esteem: Two different ways of relating to oneself. *Journal of Personality*, 77(1), 23-50.

Nicol, D. J., & Macfarlane-Dick, D. (2006). Formative assessment and self-regulated learning: A model and seven principles of good feedback practice. *Studies in Higher Education*, 31(2), 199–218.

Nieto, S. (2010). *Language, culture, and teaching: Critical perspectives for a new century*. Routledge.

Noguera, P., & Wing, J. Y. (2016). *Unfinished business: Closing the achievement gap in our nation's schools.* San Francisco: Jossey-Bass.

O'Connor, K. (2019*). A repair kit for grading: Fifteen fixes for broken grades.* Pearson.

Ogbu, J. U. (1992). Understanding cultural diversity and learning. *Educational Researcher*, 21(8), 5–14. doi: 10.3102/0013189X021008005

Okonofua, J. A., Paunesku, D., & Walton, G. M. (2016). Brief intervention to encourage empathic discipline cuts suspension rates in half among adolescents. *Proceedings of the National Academy of Sciences*, 113 (19), 5221-5226.

Okonofua, J. A., Walton, G. M., & Eberhardt, J. L. (2016). A Vicious Cycle: A Social-Psychological Account of Extreme Racial Disparities in School Discipline. *Perspectives on Psychological Science*, 11(3), 381–398. https://doi.org/10.1177/1745691616635592

Owens, D., & Lynch, J. (2012). Multidimensional approaches to educational disadvantage and their implications for policy. *Policy Futures in Education*, 10(1), 114–127. doi: 10.2304/pfie.2012.10.1.114

Pekrun, R., Elliot, A. J., & Maier, M. A. (2017). Achievement goals and achievement emotions: Testing a model of their joint relations with academic performance. *Journal of Educational Psychology*, 109(3), 377-394.

Pekrun, R., Frenzel, A. C., Goetz, T., & Perry, R. P. (2007). The control-value theory of achievement emotions: An integrative approach to emotions in education. *In Emotion in education* (pp. 13-36). Academic Press.

Pekrun, R., & Linnenbrink-Garcia, L. (2014). *International Handbook of Emotions in Education.* Routledge.

References

Pettigrew, T. F., & Tropp, L. R. (2006). A meta-analytic test of intergroup contact theory. *Journal of Personality and Social Psychology*, 90(5), 751-783. doi:10.1037/0022-3514.90.5.751

Portes, A., & Rumbaut, R. G. (2014). *Immigrant America: A portrait, updated, and expanded.* DOI: https://doi.org/10.1525/9780520959156.

Purdie-Vaughns, V., & Eibach, R. P. (2008). Intersectional invisibility: The distinctive advantages and disadvantages of multiple subordinate-group identities. *Sex roles*, pp. 59, 377–391.

Reardon, S. F., Kalogrides, D., & Shores, K. (2018). The geography of racial/ethnic test score gaps. *Educational Researcher*, 47(6), 320–334.

Reardon, S. F., & Portilla, X. A. (2016). Recent trends in income, racial, and ethnic school readiness gaps at kindergarten entry. *Aera Open*, 2(3), 2332858416657343.

Reeve, J. (2012). *A self-determination theory perspective on student engagement. In handbook of research on student engagement* (pp. 149–172). Boston, MA: Springer US.

Reid, W. J., & Albee, G. W. (1999). The advocacy coalition: A collaborative approach to school, family, and community empowerment. *Journal of Educational and Psychological Consultation*, 10(4), 297-312.

Romero, A. J., & Roberts, R. E. (2003). Perception of discrimination and ethnocultural variables in a diverse group of adolescents. *Journal of Adolescence*, 26(3), 331–346. https://doi.org/10.1016/S0140-1971(03)00011-4

Roorda, D. L., Koomen, H. M. Y., Spilt, J. L., & Oort, F. J. (2011). The influence of affective teacher-student relationships on students' school engagement and achievement: A meta-analytic approach. *Review of Educational Research*, 81(4), 493-529.

Roosevelt, T. (1910). *Citizenship in a Republic.* Speech delivered at the Sorbonne, Paris, France.

Rosen, L. D., Carrier, L. M., & Cheever, N. A. (2013). Facebook and texting made me do it: Media-induced task-switching while studying. *Computers in Human Behavior*, 29(3), 948-958.

Rosenthal, R., & Jacobson, L. (1968). *Pygmalion in the classroom: Teacher expectation and pupils' intellectual development*. Holt, Rinehart, and Winston.

Rumberger, R. W. (2011). *Dropping Out: Why Students Drop Out of High School and What Can Be Done About It*. Harvard University Press.

Rusbult, C. E., Martz, J. M., & Agnew, C. R. (1998). The Investment Model Scale: Measuring commitment level, satisfaction level, quality of alternatives, and investment size. *Personal Relationships*, 5(4), 357-391.

Ryan, R. M., & Deci, E. L. (2000a). Intrinsic and extrinsic motivations: Classic definitions and new directions. *Contemporary Educational Psychology*, 25(1), 54-67. https://doi.org/10.1006/ceps.1999.1020

Ryan, R. M., & Deci, E. L. (2000b). Self-determination theory and the facilitation of intrinsic motivation, social development, and well-being. *American Psychologist*, 55(1), 68-78. doi: 10.1037/0003-066X.55.1.68

Santa-Ramirez, S. (2022). Sink or swim: The mentoring experiences of Latinx PhD students with faculty of color. *Journal of Diversity in Higher Education*, 15(1), 124–134. https://doi.org/10.1037/dhe0000335

Scarcella, R. C., & Oxford, R. L. (1992). *The tapestry of language learning: The individual in the communicative classroom*. Boston: Heinle & Heinle.

Schein, E. H. (2010). *Organizational culture and leadership*. John Wiley & Sons.

Schneider, M., & Preckel, F. (2017). Variables associated with achievement in higher education: A systematic review of meta-analyses. *Psychological Bulletin*, 143(6), 565-600.

Schumacher, R., Smith, J. A., & Mehus, C. J. (2018). *Trauma-informed schools: A practice guide*. National Child Traumatic Stress Network.

References

Schwartz, O. S., Dudgeon, P., Sheeber, L., & Yap, M. B. H. (2012). Intimacy as a mediator of the relationship between depressive symptoms and problematic interpersonal behaviors in adolescence. *Journal of Youth and Adolescence*, 41(11), 1444-1458.

Senge, P. M. (1990). *The fifth discipline: The art and practice of the learning organization*. Doubleday/Currency.

Simpkins, S. D., Davis-Kean, P. E., Eccles, J. S., & Mathews, J. S. (2013). The power of peers: The effects of social group membership on academic engagement and achievement. *Journal of Adolescent Research*, 28(2), 166–186.

Skiba, R. J., Arredondo, M. I., & Williams, N. T. (2011a). More than a metaphor: The contribution of exclusionary discipline to a school-to-prison pipeline. *Equity & Excellence in Education*, 44(4), 451-471.

Skiba, R. J., Knesting, K., & Ronfeldt, M. (2002). Zero Tolerance, Zero Evidence: An Analysis of School Disciplinary Practice. *Policy Research Report #SRS2*. Indiana Education Policy Center.

Skinner, B. F. (1965). *Science and human behavior (No. 92904)*. Simon and Schuster.

Solórzano, D., Ceja, M., & Yosso, T. (2000). Critical race theory, racial microaggressions, and campus racial climate: The experiences of African American college students. *Journal of Negro Education*, 69(1/2), 60–73.

Steele, C. M. (1997). A threat in the air: How stereotypes shape intellectual identity and performance. *American Psychologist*, 52(6), 613–629. doi: 10.1037/0003-066X.52.6.613

Steele, C. M. (2010). *Whistling Vivaldi: How stereotypes affect us and what we can do*. W. W. Norton & Company.

Steele, C. M., & Aronson, J. (1995). Stereotype threat and the intellectual test performance of African Americans. *Journal of Personality and Social Psychology*, 69(5), 797–811. doi: 10.1037/0022-3514.69.5.797

Suarez-Orozco, C., Suarez-Orozco, M. M., & Todorova, I. (2010). *Learning a new land: Immigrant students in American society*. Harvard University Press.

Suárez-Orozco, M. M., & Suárez-Orozco, C. (2001). *Children of immigration*.

Cambridge, MA: Harvard University Press.

Sugai, G., Horner, R. H., Dunlap, G., Hieneman, M., Lewis, T. J., Nelson, C. M., Scott, T., Liaupsin, C., Sailor, W., Turnbull, A. P., Turnbull, H. R., Wickham, D., Wilcox, B., & Zirkel, P. A. (2010). Applying Positive Behavior Support and Functional Behavioral Assessment in Schools. *Journal of Positive Behavior Interventions*, 2(3), 131–143. https://doi.org/10.1177/109830070000200302

Suldo, S. M., Thalji-Raitano, A., Kiefer, S. M., & Ferron, J. M. (2016). Conceptualizing high school students' mental health through a dual-factor model. *School Psychology Review*, 45(4), 434-457.

Sutcher, L., Darling-Hammond, L., & Carver-Thomas, D. (2016). *A coming crisis in teaching? Teacher supply, demand, and shortages in the U.S. Learning Policy Institute.*

Tangney J. P., Baumeister R. F., & Boone A. L. (2004). High self-control predicts good adjustment, less pathology, better grades, and interpersonal success. *Journal of Personality*, 72, 271–324. 10.1111/j.0022-3506.2004.00263.x

Thapa, A., Cohen, J., Guffey, S., & Higgins-D'Alessandro, A. (2013). A review of school climate research. *Review of Educational Research*, 83(3), 357-385. https://doi.org/10.3102/0034654313483907

Thompson, S. J., & Vaughn, S. (2002). Bilingualism and special education: Issues in assessment and pedagogy. *Dyslexia*, 8(4), 234–248.

Tice, D. M., & Bratslavsky, E. (2000). Giving in to feel good: The place of emotion regulation in the context of general self-control. *Psychological Inquiry*, 11(3), 149–159.

Tomlinson, C. A., Brighton, C., Hertberg, H., Callahan, C. M., Moon, T. R., Brimijoin, K., Conover, L. A., & Reynolds, T. (2003). Differentiating instruction in response to student readiness, interest, and learning profile in academically diverse classrooms: A review of literature. *Journal for the Education of the Gifted*, 27(2-3), pp. 119–145.

References

Tucker, C. M., Herman, K. C., Weddington, L. E., Grogan-Kaylor, A., & Linder, N. J. (2019). Teacher cultural competence and its association with classroom peer aggression and victimization. *School Psychology Quarterly*, 34(1), 44–56.

Turner, B. J., & Butler, M. J. (2003). Direct and indirect effects of stress on nonsuicidal self-injury. *Journal of Youth and Adolescence*, 32(4), 259–267.

U.S. Department of Education. (2018). *School climate and discipline: Resources to promote safe and supportive schools.* https://www2.ed.gov/policy/gen/guid/school-discipline/files/school-climate-and-discipline-guidance-package.pdf

Vohs, K. D., Baumeister, R. F., Schmeichel, B. J., Twenge, J. M., Nelson, N. M., & Tice, D. M. (2013). Making choices impairs subsequent self-control: A limited-resource account of decision making, self-regulation, and active initiative. *Motivation and Emotion*, 37(4), 684-701.

Vroom, V. H. (1964). *Work and motivation.* John Wiley & Sons.

Wachtel, T. (2013). *Real Justice: How We Can Revolutionize Our Response to Wrongdoing.* The New Press.

Walton, G. M., & Cohen, G. L. (2011). A brief social-belonging intervention improves academic and health outcomes of minority students. *Science*, p. 331, 1447–1451. doi:10.1126/science.1198364

Warschauer, M., & Matuchniak, T. (2010). New technology and digital worlds: Analyzing evidence of equity in access, use, and outcomes. *Review of research in education*, 34(1), 179-225.

Wentzel, K. R. (1999). Social-motivational processes and interpersonal relationships: Implications for understanding motivation at school. *Journal of Educational Psychology*, 91(1), 76-97.

Wentzel, K. R. (2016). Teacher-student relationships. In Handbook of motivation at school (pp. 211-230). Routledge.

Wormeli, R. (2006). *Fair Isn't Always Equal: Assessing & Grading in the Differentiated Classroom.* Stenhouse Publishers.

Yeager, D. S., & Dweck, C. S. (2012). Mindsets that promote resilience: When students believe that personal characteristics can be developed. *Educational Psychologist*, 47(4), 302-314. doi:10.1080/00461520.2012.722805

Youniss, J., McLellan, J. A., & Yates, M. (1997). What we know about engendering civic identity. *American Behavioral Scientist*, 40(6), 620–631.

Zimmerman, B. J. (2000). Attaining self-regulation: A social cognitive perspective. In M. Boekaerts, P. R. Pintrich, & M. Zeidner (Eds.), *Handbook of self-regulation* (pp. 13–39). Academic Press.

Zimmerman, B. J. (2008). Investigating self-regulation and motivation: Historical background, methodological developments, and future prospects. *American Educational Research Journal*, 45(1), 166-183. https://doi.org/10.3102/0002831207312909

Zimmerman, B. J. (2019). *Self-regulated learning: Theories, measures, and outcomes.* In J. Dunlosky & K. A. Rawson (Eds.), The Cambridge handbook of cognition and education (pp. 274-298). Cambridge University Press.

Zins, J. E., Bloodworth, M. R., Weissberg, R. P., & Walberg, H. J. (2007). The scientific base linking social and emotional learning to school success. *Journal of Educational and Psychological Consultation*, 17(2-3), 191-210.